# introduction

I started working on this issue in mid-October. The first draft of the introduction sounded bleak. How could it not? These are dystopian times. I decided to wait until after the election to finish the introduction.

It is now mid-November, and President-Elect Biden is putting together a coronavirus task force. Vice President-Elect Harris has shattered a glass ceiling. Trump is deranged and refusing to concede. Four Seasons Total Landscaping and Gritty have brought joy to the land. The pandemic is ravaging the world, particularly the US. Hope was missing in October, but it is there again, despite everything.

In my personal life, several family members are dealing with health issues, my co-workers are struggling from unrelenting pressures and anxiety, and some of my zine friends are also suffering. Over and over during the last four years, and particularly the last eight months, what matters has come down to one thing – we have to take care of one another.

Wear a goddamned mask. Check in on people. Offer support. Ask for support. Help where you can, how you can. Tip your delivery people. Shop local. Compliment others (in a non-creepy way). Build people up. Support artists, writers, caregivers, essential workers, parents, children, and anyone else who needs it. But fuck the racists and hatemongers – don't help them, let them suffer.

The only way we are going to recover from COVID-19 is to protect other people as much as, if not more than, we protect ourselves. The same goes for recovering from the Trump administration. We need to fight for one another. We have so much work do to.

A number of zines reviewed within this issue were written during the pandemic. Personally, it helped me to hear other people talk about what has been going on this year. It looks like we're going into what will likely be a long, hard winter of lockdowns and isolation. It is a good time to write a few letters, order a few zines, send some trades, and maybe write a zine or two. Be part of the hope and connection we so desperately need right now.

Take care,
Davida

**Penthouse L, 1170 Ocean Parkway, Brooklyn, NY 11230**

## zines & hometowns

I've been making zines for some time now; my very first one was **ROLLER SPORTS REPORT**, which the original editor offered to me in 1985. Although I enjoyed producing it, there was always something in the back of my mind that nagged at me. One day I realized what it was: I wanted something that I originated by myself. So I started thinking about what interested me the most. And the answer was (the envelope, please) ...my hometown! Brooklyn, New York has almost 400 years of history under its belt. It's big enough to be a city on its own, and, in fact, until a (rigged) election in 1895, it was. And there certainly weren't any other zines about Brooklyn, so why not one from me? I created my first issue in 1991, and it's been off to the races since then.

In all these years I've been doing the zine – and trading with others – something else has nagged at me: there are review zines, perzines, poetry zines, political zines, litzines, and pretty much any other topic you can think of, but there are hardly any hometown zines. I find this almost completely incomprehensible. Some years ago, I traded for a zine called **ISOLATION RANCH**. It was a hometown zine from a guy who lived in a tiny town in the middle of the Nevada desert. I really liked it, and I was sad when it ceased publication. These days, there's **GENEVA13**, devoted to the city of Geneva, in upstate New York. But offhand, I can't think of any others.

My potentially impertinent question is, why aren't there more hometown zines? I should think that more people would be fascinated by the place they call home. You don't need to live in a huge city. No place isn't interesting. Get a map of your city or town. Aren't you curious about street names? If there are streets that don't conform to a grid, don't you wonder why? You can be sure there's a good reason! And while you can tell me there aren't interesting things to see scattered all over the place, I won't believe you. Shouldn't you investigate some of them?

The fact that you're reading this now means that you're not unfamiliar with zines. Might you be inspired to start a hometown zine of your own? If this essay opens the floodgates to hometown zines around the world (if not the country), I hope you'll also want to trade for mine. This could cause a larger expenditure in the postal area than I was probably anticipating, but I think I could manage it.

**2140 Erma Dr.,**
**East Meadow, NY 11554**
**Passscribe@aol.com**
**kenbausertsnostalgicmuseum.blogspot.com/**
**thekenbausertchronicles.blogspot.com/**

# ken's column

## THE PRINTER PARADOX

Printers are the lifeblood of zinesters who produce their work on paper, whether you do it yourself or bring it to a commercial shop to have it done. Back in a previous issue of my **KEN CHRONICLES**, I wrote about how my old Sharp AL 1610 copy machine needed toner and a drum – and how expensive the parts were because that machine was so old, and everybody who had parts for it was price gouging. So I bought a discontinued Canon MF244dw black-and-white laser scanner/copier/printer for $142, and it produced great output. The only problem was that the toner cartridges were super expensive and didn't last as long as I thought they would.

I never use compatible ink in my ink jet printers, so when I needed toner for the laser printer, I bought only a genuine Canon cartridge. Although most sellers charge about $90 each, I was able to find better prices from eBay vendors that were about $20 less. However, I read some feedback from other users of the Canon lasers that spoke highly of compatible toner cartridges that were about 80% cheaper than the genuine Canon and produced equally fine output. Figuring I was going to go broke if I continued using the expensive stuff, I ordered two of the cheap cartridges to try them out.

Guess what? They worked just fine.

The scene now moves to our condo in Florida, where someone gave me an old HP ink jet printer/scanner/copier for free. I originally thought I didn't need a printer while in Florida, but after spending seven weeks there in the fall and four months in the winter, I really appreciated being able to scan, copy, and print (especially since I'm on the Board of Directors of our Condo Association). Since the HP refused to take compatible ink cartridges, I found some cheap Genuine ink on eBay, and those worked great. The trouble was that the printer itself was finicky, didn't work properly half the time, and the ink would dry up during the five months of not being used during summer, when I wasn't in Florida. Finally, the HP printer refused to work at all, and I threw it into one of our community dumpsters.

Since the laser printer toner doesn't mind when you don't use it for long periods of time, I looked into buying a cheap laser printer for our condo. The Apple laptop computer I use in Florida was a gift from someone who bought a new one. The operating system is an older version, but – although kind of slow – it works just fine; besides, it's actually the latest OS that this MacBook will support. So any printer I looked at had to work with my older software. Luckily, I discovered a brand-new (but older model) MF232dw of the same type Canon laser printer I use in New York. And because it was manufactured in 2013, it was compatible with my laptop and was really cheap; Walmart online had it for $99, with free next-day delivery to our condo. I figured they wouldn't have a model this old in any of their stores, so I wondered how they could make that claim. Anyway, I ordered it. I received a confirmation email that said the printer would be delivered the next day by FedEx.

I stayed around our condo the next day, wanting to be home for the delivery. At 2:15 p.m., I received an email from FedEx saying my printer had been delivered. Figuring that the delivery guy left it downstairs by our car port I went to look, but found nothing. Since our building contains four condos, I checked with my neighbors, but the printer was nowhere to be found. So I call Walmart to report the problem, and the girl tells me, "Okay, we'll send you out a new one."

"A new one? Why don't you try and find out what happened to the first one?"

She gives me a case number and tells me to call FedEx. When I call FedEx, they say they'll check into it. Give them two days, they say. So after two days, the people at FedEx have no answers for me. I am not believing what's happening by now. I tell the woman at FedEx, "Can't you just ask the driver what he did with the printer? Are you people totally crazy over there, or just incompetent?"

They do nothing for me, and tell me to call Walmart and ask for another printer. Shaking my head in disbelief at this whole experience, I call Walmart and relay the whole sordid story. After all is said and done, they tell me they don't have another printer and they're issuing me a refund.

By now, I just want a new printer and am done playing games with Walmart and FedEx. So, I go online again and find only one other store that has that printer for a cheap price: Best Buy. Of course, they don't have it in any of their stores, but their price is $99.99 and they'll ship it to me for free within a week.

But a funny thing happened while I was checking out with the online purchase: the transaction was now being handled by Google. I guess Best Buy and Google have some kind of partnering agreement. And, since this was my first online purchase through Google, they were offering me $10 off. Okay, this tale just gets weirder as we move further along but, yes, I pay the cheaper price for the printer and am told that FedEx is going to deliver it. That's right... FedEx!

As the days go by, I receive an email from FedEx that says the printer will be delivered by 4:17 p.m. on Tuesday. Don't ask me how they can pinpoint a delivery down to a specific minute, because it's just another crazy piece of the puzzle, okay? I stick around the condo all day that Tuesday, 4:17 p.m. comes and goes, and there's no printer. So I look at my emails to make sure there's not one saying it was delivered, and I notice the original confirmation email was sent from their office in the Central Time Zone. "Maybe that means it will arrive by 5:17 p.m. Eastern Time," I'm thinking.

Lo and behold, at 5:00 p.m., I hear a truck outside. Looking out the window though, I'm disappointed to see it's a UPS truck. But, what's that I hear... footsteps on the stairs leading up to our place? Yes, it's the UPS man carrying my Canon laser printer. As I open the door I say, "This was supposed to be delivered by FedEx; how is it you've got it?"

The guy looks at me like I've got two heads and says, "Hey, all I know is... it's on my truck and I'm told to deliver it."

You can't make this stuff up.

**115 Irving Street**
**Laurel, MD 20707-4503**
**markellorhighwater@gmail.com**

# phrase anatomy

### CONSCIENTIOUS OBJECTION

When I was a college freshman at Georgetown University, I took an English class with my friend Dora. Dr. Roland Flint assigned frequent essays and gave us demerits for grammatical errors. I was horrified to learn that Dora lost points for splitting an infinitive. For example, Star Trek would have gotten points off for saying "to boldly go where no man has gone before," instead of "to go boldly where no man has gone before."

Since Professor Flint gave us extra credit for what he called "optional extra papers," I wrote about the fact that splitting an infinitive is frowned upon only because the first English grammar book was a translation from a Latin grammar book – and that Latin infinitives simply cannot be split. I've always liked the idea of splitting infinitives, since it puts the modifier right smack in the middle of the verb, so it's clearly modifying the verb itself.

I got an "A" for my optional extra paper, but Dora didn't get her points back. When

I asked why not, he said "Dora didn't write this – you did."

As I was considering writing "he said, 'Dora didn't write this,'" with the comma, I decided to omit the comma before Dora's name. Our beloved professor is long gone, but he might approve of my decision. A quotation is the direct object of the verb. I wouldn't write I ate, an apple, so I shouldn't write he said, "Dora didn't write this."

On one of my essays for Dr. Flint, I left the strip of paper between the spiral binding and the perforations in my notebook. I wrote "optional extra paper" on it. I was hoping to get extra credit for that. I did not.

However, although Dora is skeptical of this, I believe he would agree with me that it's OK to consistently use whatever grammar rules you like, as long as you believe in them.

## jeff somers

**PO Box 3024, Hoboken, NJ 07030**
**mreditor@innerswine.com**
**www.innerswine.com**

# it means it's wank

*"So what does that mean? It means it's wank." — Vic Flange, www.fleshmouth.co.uk [now defunct], describing my zine.*

### THE ART OF NOT RECOGNIZING YOURSELF

In which your humble correspondent ponders the fact that he can't remember any of the things that he wrote so passionately about in his zine.

FRIENDOS, I have a bad memory. It's hard to explain; the past is a distant place for me, blurry and often completely blank. I forget a remarkable amount of stuff. I can't remember what people looked like, I can't remember what I did twenty, thirty, four years ago. Sometimes I come across photos and stare at them, literally at a loss. I mean, I remember stuff, but not well. Everything kind of gets fuzzy.

I actually think it helps my writing. Because I can't really remember details, I'm not locked into reality or haunted by my inability to capture it, giving me a lot of flexibility to convey the emotional point without being bogged down by the facts. But it also leads to some strange moments of dissonance, like when I read something I wrote in my zine **THE INNER SWINE** a long time ago and not only don't remember anything that's discussed, but don't really recognize the person who wrote it.

## MATH IS HARD

In which your humble correspondent struggles with the economics of zine publishing.

FRIENDOS, when I was a youth in fifth grade, I imagined myself something of a math genius. Kids are dumb, and one of the reasons kids are dumb is that we just can't grasp the true complexity of things. So the fact that I had mastered some multiplication tables and could do long division made me a pretty smug bastard.

I was also, I realize now, always destined to create a zine, because I spent a lot of my childhood making proto-zines. For example, in seventh grade I got together with some friends and we wrote a rulebook for a role-playing game inspired by Dungeons & Dragons. It was called "Infiltrate", and it was a James Bond-ian spy RPG. I typed up the rules in the same format as the D&D rulebooks and created a cover out of construction paper. The game never caught on, but for a few short weeks the three of us thought we were going to be millionaire nerds.

Another example came a few years before, when I was the aforementioned smug bastard about my hella math skills: I actually wrote a guide for kids struggling with math, in which I explained my incredible mental powers and how anyone could use the same techniques that I used to get an A+ on grammar school-level math quizzes.

Yes, I was 100% that bitch.

It's hilarious to me today, of course, because as I gradually moved past math basics into slightly (and I cannot emphasize the use of the word "slightly" enough) more advanced mathematical subjects, I quickly realized I'd badly miscalculated. By the time I was sitting in a pre-calculus class in high school, I was in a flopsweat of panic because numbers were no longer my friends.

Which brings me to my old zine.

## A GODDAMNED BARGAIN

When I launched my zine, **THE INNER SWINE**, I arbitrarily priced it at $2 an issue (with "a goddamned bargain" written next to it, because it was), with a $5 annual subscription (for most of the run, I put out 4 issues a year, so the subscription was a good deal). As I was putting the first issue together, I knew I didn't want to give it away, because even as a confused and slightly pudgy man-child I knew that my work had value, and I wanted to at least gesture at this standard. But I also had no idea how much I should actually charge, because, as mentioned, math had become increasingly mysterious to me.

On the one hand, I was making most of the photocopies of the zine at my place of employment, so overhead was relatively low. On the other hand, copies weren't the only expense. There was postage, stock for the covers, envelopes, and other miscellaneous things. Long story short, my zine bled money from the first issue.

This isn't unusual, I suspect; I can't be the only zine publisher less concerned with turning a profit than in getting my zine out there—hell, a lot of zine-makers give their zines away. I sent copies to anyone who traded or asked for one, I kept fulfilling lapsed subscriptions for years, I took consignment deals from Tower Magazine and Desert Moon Periodicals, which meant a large portion of the issues I sent simply got mulched. I very quickly gave up making any attempt to square up accounts: I just published issues, spent what needed to be spent, and then cried into my bowls of cheap ramen and hoped to be paid in glowing reviews and zine cred. At one point, I began offering lifetime subscriptions for $50, which were surprisingly popular but also a lesson in short-term gains—sure, getting $50 in the mail was always nice, but I lost money on every single one of those deals.

Money's not everything. If I knew anything about math or finance I probably wouldn't be a writer, as it's a terrible way to make a living. But I'll also never forget the thrill of going to my P.O. Box and finding a few envelopes with wrinkled dollar bills inside along with a scrawled address. The fact that complete strangers sent me cash in the U.S. mail with the full confidence that I would fulfill their zine wishes remains a minor miracle, and one I'm not sad I participated in.

Now, if you'll excuse me, I have to research whether I can sue people who got more than four issues for $5 back in 2005.

# the **reviews**

**PO Box 877**
**Lansdowne, PA 19050**
**syndprod@gmail.com**
**instagram/twitter: @syndprod**

**BASIC PAPER AIRPLANE #13: THE CASSETTE TAPE ISSUE**

Available from Antiquated Future (antiquatedfuture.com)
Price: $5 / Trades: Unknown
Size: 5.5" x 8.5" / Pages: 60

C30-C60-C90 Go! Twenty contributors on the unassuming cassette tape. Prerecorded tapes are a large part of my musical history, including many from the "3 for $10" table at Listening Booth, like *The Velvet Underground & Nico*, the soundtrack to the Sting movie *Brimstone & Treacle*, the Beatles "Rock and Roll" collections, the Proclaimers, Hoodoo Gurus, and many more. It's heartwarming to see albums on cassette getting love in this zine. The issue also includes pieces by people who run cassette-only record labels, concert bootleggers, and musicians doing sound experiments on lo-fi cassette recording decks. As expected, there are also essays on mix tapes, either recorded from the radio or made for others. In all, a great variety of voices about those little plastic rectangles. Recommended.

**THE COURTROOM ARTIST RESIDENCY REPORT: RESIDENCIES #13-#16**

Marc Fischer/Public Collectors
publiccollectors.org
Half Letter Press, PO Box 12588,
Chicago, IL 60612
halfletterpress.com
Price: $7 / Trades: Unknown
Size: 7" x 8.5" / Pages: 40

The title implies this is a zine about residencies for artists who do the drawings in courtrooms, but it's a completely different, unique project. These "residencies" are one-day events where Marc Fischer of Public Collectors takes an artist of any sort (writer, visual artist, musician) to observe court proceedings at the Cook County Criminal Court in Chicago, and then to lunch at Tacqueria El Milango to discuss the day.

Courtrooms are public spaces where everyday citizens can come in and watch proceedings, except for closed courtrooms (family and juvenile cases). Most people aren't aware of this, and it's something people in the United States need to know more about. The courts in the U.S. are intentionally secretive and confusing. Most people only see what happens in a courtroom in television shows and movies, during jury duty, and maybe if they have committed a crime.

Marc's interviews with the four artists (Imani Elizabeth Jackson, Lucas Reif, Salome Chasnoff, and Tom Burtonwood) are insightful, discussing the cases they observed, individual judges' personalities, and the Chicago justice system. This is a thoughtful zine about something I have never had to ever think about. When Philadelphia courts are back to in-person work, I'm curious to observe a courtroom for the day, thanks to reading this zine.

**CUL DE SAC #8: PAST LIVES**

Liz Mason and Julie Halpern
PO Box 477553, Chicago, IL 60647
lizmasonzines.etsy.com
Available from Quimby's (quimbys.com)
Price: $4 / Trades: Inquire
Size: 5.5" x 8.5" / Pages: 36

The estimable Liz Mason and Julie Halpern restarted **CUL DE SAC** after a long hiatus, and are keeping it going with their second issue since resurrection. It's an excellent co-authored, quirky perzine, with each lady writing about the obsessions and remembrances of things past. Liz recalls dumping someone who didn't like *The Matrix*, and Julie writes about attending many, many *Supernatural* fan conventions (the show, not the concept), what it means to her, the ridiculous cost of photo ops, and panels consisting of "that one guy who played that one demon in that one episode." In the "things that aren't there anymore" category, Liz laments the loss of beloved hangout the Bagel Restaurant & Deli in Skokie, IL, and Julie the closing of Toys R Us. Best friends since childhood, hopefully Liz and Julie will keep publishing **CUL DE SAC** on a regular basis. This zine is like reconnecting with long-ago friends, and talking for hours as if no time passed.

**THE HAPPY LONER #12**

Izalixe Straightheart
izart.etsy.com
izalixe@gmail.com
Price: $5US / $4 Can / $6 ROW
Size: 5.5" x 8.5" / Pages: 24

*"For now I am just a visitor but I am not a tourist. I know this place, inside and out."*

Iza Straightheart is a French-Canadian woman who is fortunate to live in Vancouver, BC, for several months every year because she can do her work from any location. This issue includes a helpful map of free things in the city (eg, libraries, Little Free Libraries, Wi-Fi, etc), essays about being French-Canadian (the rest of the year Iza lives in Quebec), an essay on time (which I don't agree with), and media reviews, including YouTuber reviews, something I had never seen before in a zine. Iza's writing seemed oddly familiar to me, so I did some digging and found I'd read her work a long time ago in a cross-Canadian tour diary following her favorite band (at the time), Moist. She's also a prolific YouTuber under username "izalixe".

**IF ANIMALS COULD TALK COLORING BOOK: A QUARANTINE DISTRACTION**

Carla Butwin and Josh Cassidy
Available from Microcosm Publishing
(microcosmpublishing.com/catalog/zines/13474)
Price: $7.95 / Size: 7" x 8.5" / Pages: 28

Because of crappy eyesight and caffeine consumption, I never got into the "adult coloring book" trend because the designs are usually detailed drawings with teeny-tiny spaces. I don't want to press my nose to the paper and constantly sharpen pencils to color in a picture I don't care about. However, **IF ANIMALS COULD TALK** has large, clean, airy drawings of animals by Carla Butwin and Josh Cassidy to color in any way you want. They comment on the pandemic! "I heard the whole thing started in a lab", the rat says. A bird insists, "I'm telling ya... it's the 5G." And a killer bee wonders, "Wait, what the fuck is a murder hornet?" Not for kids, and a great distraction for when you get tired of puzzles, trying to bake bread, and screaming into the void.

**IS IT JUST ME OR ARE WE NAILING THIS? ESSAYS ON BOJACK HORSEMAN**

Available from Antiquated Future
(antiquatedfuture.com)
Price: $5 / Size: 5.5" x 8.5: / Pages: 68

Since the series ended in January 2020, expect a flurry of academic press books about *Bojack Horseman* around mid-2021, filled with observations comparing the show to dense, pretentious concepts. But why wait? For a more personal approach than the future academic tomes, pick up this thick zine, with essays written by people deeply moved by this complex show. It has a range of features about *Bojack Horseman*, not all of them focusing on its nihilistic bleakness. For example, Joshua James Amberson considers two minor characters that appeared in the final season as a perfect example of the screwball comedies of the 1940s. (Many people hated gossip journalists Paige and Max, but if you got the reference, they were fun.) There's an interview with the curator of the Instagram account @BojackHiddenJokes, fan art, Bojack tarot, and quote collections. At the core of **IS IT JUST ME OR ARE WE NAILING THIS?** are the deeply personal essays relating with individual characters: the damaged, addicted Bojack; the hardworking, long-suffering, ever-disappointed Princess Carolyn; the no-nonsense but conflicted Diane.

The essay "The Myth of Todd Chavez: Hollywood's Absurd Hero", by Tessa Livingstone, put the seemingly shiftless slacker character into focus for me, after years of not understanding him. According to her, Todd beautifully embodies Camus's philosophy of the absurd. Instead of viewing Todd as comic relief, he is totally free and embraces the weirdness of himself. I struggled with the "purpose" of Todd the first few seasons, but once he asserted himself more, appreciated him. He's also one of the few asexual characters in a television series.

This zine is highly recommended whether you've watched the entirety of *Bojack Horseman* or are a newcomer. Don't worry about spoilers, as they don't apply, and instead appreciate the measured, thoughtful appreciations.

**RAZORCAKE #117**
PO Box 42129, Los Angeles, CA 90412
razorcake.org
Price: $3 / Size: 8.5" x 11" / Pages: 112

There's not much new to say in a review of **RAZORCAKE**: inky pages, band interviews, Top 5s, record and zine reviews, columns, and ads. However, this issue is different because it was published in June 2020, deep in the middle of the coronavirus pandemic and the unrest triggered by the murder of George Floyd. The columns are lacking the usual lightness and instead center on the dreadful current events. Jennifer Whiteford compiles a great list of books for raising non-racist kids. Jim Rutland writes on police violence. Donna Ramone talks about how conspiracy theories have gone from largely harmless alien abduction fun (RIP Art Bell) to truly dangerous ideas about Covid-19, child sex rings, and crisis actors. Designated Dale chronicles his two-month bout with coronavirus, contracted early in the pandemic in March. He could barely get a test (and when he did, it took 9 days for a result), get into an urgent health clinic, or see his regular doctor. He developed bilateral pneumonia and took two trips to the ER for bags of strong IV antibiotics. He's well now, but wants to make sure readers understand: "...I've never been as sick in my whole fifty years on this earth than what I've experienced with this creepy COVID carnival of horrors." There's also the usual interviews, record reviews, ads, and a good feature on the films and career of John Waters, a punk in his own right.

**SOLD AS BLANK/POSSIBLE LOST MEDIA**
Marc Fischer/Public Collectors
publiccollectors.org
Half Letter Press, PO Box 12588,
Chicago, IL 60612
halfletterpress.com
Price: $5 / Size: 5.5" x 8.5" / Pages: 24

Another ephemera project from Public Collectors, eBay listings for home-recorded VHS tapes that for copyright reasons can't be sold for the content they contain, but can be "sold as blank". It's obvious that these tapes aren't being "sold as blank" – if someone was getting rid of used VHS tapes, why list out all their contents, including commercials? Selling these tapes as "blank" circumvents copyright rules and distributes "lost" content. For example, "This auction is for a single VHS tape, sold as blank. Features 2 hrs of a Beavis and Butthead "moron-a-thon" from Dec 1996." Most of the tapes are recorded from television, but there are listings for home movies such as "VHS - 1 used tape sold as blank 'KIM & CURTS WEDDING' tested but Unknown Content... I played the first few seconds, it was indeed an amateur camcorder wedding video. Small quaint church. I do not know how long or the rest of the content." Where did the seller find this tape? Who were Kim and Curt? These listings are more interesting than tapes of old awards shows or cable movies.

**UNF#CK YOUR YEAR**
Faith G. Harper
Available from Microcosm Publishing (microcosmpublishing.com/catalog/books/11372)
Price: $14.95 / Size: 5" x 7" / Pages: 160

I am the least appropriate person to review a self-care workbook. Raised by the Silent Generation, I've led a mostly unexamined life. I learned if you have time to worry about "who you are", you're not working hard enough and to go clean the basement. Self-reflection is something I don't do. Perhaps in a way I am the perfect person to review this "weekly unplanned and self-care activity book to manage your anxiety, depression, anger, triggers, and freak-outs."

The workbook is divided into themed seasons, such as "Life Essentials", then into months, e.g., Adulting Month, Anger Management Month, Sleep Mastery Month, Intimacy Development Month (huh?), and then into weekly activities. The planner can be started anytime since the user fills in the dates.

There's nothing too deep or extensive in **UNF#CK YOUR YEAR**. It's a variety pack of self-care, mental wellness, and coping techniques. Since I can't comment on how well it works without trying it, here is my plan: start using this book at the beginning of the next available month, use it until reviews are due for the next issue of **XD**, and then report on the experience. That's the only fair way to assess the usefulness of this book. Stay tuned.

**WE'LL NEVER HAVE PARIS #17: HINDSIGHT**
Available from Antiquated Future (antiquatedfuture.com)
Price: $6 / Size: 4.25" x 5.5" / Pages: 52

If there was fairness in the creative sphere, **WNHP** would be receiving the accolades, distribution, and financial support generally given to Dave Eggers-type concerns. For now, readers of this zine will have to make do with one excellent collection a year, smartly printed on crisp linen paper. This volume's theme is "hindsight", essays about returns and looking backwards from a varied group of contributors: a movie fan, a grad student, the founder of Quimby's bookstore, a medical student, and a former police officer, and others. Essays on bald spots, temporary deafness, core exams, movie premieres, and returning to your original profession. Cerebral and concise, another great issue of **WNHP**.

**YEAR OF ZINES!**
Sarah Mirk
Available from the author (mirkwork.com) or Antiquated Future (antiquatedfuture.com)
Price: $12 / Size: 7.5" x 10" / Pages: 224

At the beginning of 2019, visual journalist (and frequent **THE NIB** contributor) Sarah Mirk challenged herself to make a folded, eight-panel, one-sheet zine every day for a year. Sarah needed a creative outlet from the intense book project she was working on. (Note: the book is now published, *Guantanamo Voices: True Accounts from the World's Most Infamous Prison.*) She decided a one-page zine was something she could complete in about an hour, and be a good mental break. She made sure to have a clipboard with paper, pencils, and pens with her at all times so she could work anywhere: in line, on the bus, at a coffee shop. This book collects her 100 favorites from the year and range from silly to serious, informative, newsy, personal, political, self-loathing, self-loving, self-caring, and more.

Here's five of my favorites from the book:

- American Public Transit Systems as Fictional Characters
- Why is my cat crying?
- Words Book Lovers Need
- 110 Happy Things
- Know Your Varieties of Existential Crisis

**YEAR OF ZINES** is highly recommended – it's like getting 100 zines for a low price! This project has inspired me to try to make a few one-page zines I can finish in an afternoon as opposed to the weeks and months my zine projects stretch out to. I can't promise one every day, but I can try for one a week for a year.

**97 Brown Ave, Apt 2L**
**Holyoke, MA 01040**
**motes@simons-rock.edu**

---

**BROOKLYN! #109**
Fred Argoff
Penthouse L, 1170 Ocean Parkway,
Brooklyn NY 11230
Price: $10 for a 4 issue subscription (PAYMENT IN CASH! Fred adds: US currency please!)
Size: 5.5" x 8.5" / Pages: 24

**ANACHRONISMS IV**
Price: $2 (US) / Trades: Inquire
Size: 5.5" x 8.5" / Pages: 20

I sort of feel like at this point it wouldn't be an **XD** review without **BROOKLYN!**, frankly. Say it with me, people: "The name of this zine is **BROOKLYN!** and that's also what the zine is about, Fred's beloved borough of Brooklyn." **BROOKLYN!** is always a combination of history, photography, and other Brooklyn-related things, and it's a long-standing awesome series that's an interesting read even if you don't live there. It's also worth mentioning that these issues are overall just suuuuper crisp: the layout is impeccable, and Fred sticks to a pretty strict publication schedule (briefly disrupted earlier this year due to the pandemic, but as soon as copy shops were open again, **BROOKLYN!** was there).

Clearly the best way to get your **BROOKLYN!** is to get a subscription. Issues are published quarterly, so getting a whole year's worth gives you a fuller picture of what **BROOKLYN!** is and does, and sometimes that'll include special issues and surprise new series. Fred has a whole set order for the issues; some issues are photography-based (109 includes many photos), some (like 109) include one of my favorite features (the Brooklyn lexicon and pronunciation guide, which legit never fails to entertain), and then every once in a while you'll get an unexpected treat like a Brooklyn version of a fable (Here it's "Monkeys, Weasels, and Brooklyn") or a stop on the Brooklyn World Tour (Brooklyns in other places). Here's the deal: you don't have to know Brooklyn at all to enjoy the zine about all things Brooklyn. Fred has a couple of other projects as well, one of which is **ANACHRONISMS**, which is mostly a series of musings about odd or out-of-date things that Fred finds interesting and/or irritating and/or baffling (digital maps, smart cars, PageMaker, and "device dependence," to name just a few that make an appearance in **ANACHRONISMS IV**).

Always, always a fun read and worth your

time. So, whaddya waitin' for? Read some **BROOKLYN!** (and some of Fred's other projects, too) already!

**PONDER POND: A SOUP OF INTENSE THOUGHT #7 AND #8**

DB Pedlar or A.S. Cruz
25727 Cherry Hill Rd.,
Cambridge Springs, PA 16403
Price: Free for the asking / Trades: Yes
Size: 5.5" x 8.5" / Pages: 20

"Readers are at liberty to send letters, stamps, money, reference books, trades, photos, art, etc. otherwise: **PONDER POND** is free for the asking." **PONDER POND** has two goals: "to promote exercising your brain" and "to promote the lost art of letter writing." Each issue includes a review or two of various media (films, books, zines), but mostly they're questions, largely sent in by readers, designed to get you thinking – and it includes a wide range of viewpoints and responses.

With a robust Letters of Comment section, both issues include various questions to ponder sent in by readers across a pretty extreme range of topics. Fair warning: these two issues are not for the faint of heart (both include content warnings: "Some topics and answers may be disturbing. Avoid reading if you are sensitive to or troubled by graphic language or the word pictures they ma[y] produce" and, on #8 in particular: "Due to the subject matter, this issue is not suitable reading for children.") with some of the questions they tackle (one's about a certain possibly-anatomically-flavored flavor of beer, another about reproductive choice). But that's also seemingly part of the point here: to get your brain moving on some unconventional questions.

**SEEDS OF SPRING #1: A MI'KMAQ TEEN DISCOVERS KROPOTKIN, PUNK, AND HER PLACE IN THE WORLD**

Written by Chris Coquard / Illustrated by Sacha Ravenda
Available through Microcosm Publishing:
Microcosm Publishing, 2752 N Williams Ave, Portland, OR 97227
https://microcosmpublishing.com/catalog/zines/10448
Price: $4.99 / Size: 10.125" x 6.625" / Pages: 34

From the back cover: "In this innovative serial graphic novel, Naguset, a modern Canadian Mi'kmaq teenager, exchanges books and mix tapes with her pen pal, Chris. Her imagination sparks when he sends her a biography of the 19th century Russian anarchist Peter Kropotkin. The story juxtaposes Naguset's personal and political coming-of-age in her loving family home with Kropotkin's rocky upbringing in a princely palace.

"These two stories of eventful lives and bold hearts are interwoven with Kropotkin's theories of freedom, Mi'kmaq vocabulary and social history, and an uplifting punk soundtrack, creating a unique reading experience bound to inspire readers to think in new ways about the issues of our time."

This issue is part of a 15-issue series that follows the main character, Naguset. One of the things I think is particularly cool about this series is that part of the proceeds go to support the Mi'gmaq-Mi'kmaq Online Talking Dictionary (so you can actually look up and hear the pronunciation of the words in this series!) at https://www.mikmaqonline.org – and there are a number of other companion resources (including the aforementioned soundtrack) and acknowledgments listed on the facing page in the issue. It's really amazing and gives a depth to this publication that's particularly fascinating and important. It's a story about self-discovery, but also about learning about your own story and where you come from – about history and about family. Issue #2 is also done, and there's a subscription service available as well through the publisher. (You can also check out their social media here: https://www.facebook.com/Seeds-Of-Spring-109073480933632.)

### THE 50 FLIP EXPERIMENT (#25 / MARCH 2020)

Dan Hill
1429 W. Lunt Ave Apt 101, Chicago IL 60626
danhill@50flipexperiment.com
50flipexperiment.com
Price: $5 US / Trades: Yes
Size: 10.25" x 6.5" / Pages: 28

Well, this one is pretty weird. There's space and a toaster and a broken teleporter. Anyway, according to the sheet that arrived with the issue: "Issue 25 is about coming to terms with one's self and making peace with the world as it is and finding beauty in stuff. It is the first part of a three-part saga. The character goes on a hike to a monastery and gets into a brief random encounter. At the end she contacts an android who may have the key to help her with her problem."

"Rated PG for thematic elements (weird, but basically fine)" – but, since that warning was included on the cover, there is one f-bomb in the closing remarks at the end of the book, though I'm not sure if kiddos-at-the-PG-level would read this publication? Maybe? I might put it more at PG-13 – guns and animal death in a hunting context, bugs mating, an owlbear (yeah, I know – it's kind of exactly what it sounds like) attacking the main character and then a prominent butthole as it runs away. But, yeah, weird's a good word to describe this storyline.

Subscriptions and back issues are both available; issue 19 is apparently about a seabeast, 22 has cowboys, and issue 24 involves a Victorian lady who gets power armor. The website includes scans of the various issues, so if you want to get a firsthand look at the art and composition style, the website is the place to check out.

I also don't yet know what the **50 FLIP EXPERIMENT** means, exactly. Will there be 50 issues? What's the Flip part? Mysteries abound…

### QUEER ANIMALS COLORING ZINE

Written by Otter Lieffe/ Illustrated by Anja van Geert
Available through Microcosm Publishing:
Microcosm Publishing,
2752 N Williams Ave, Portland, OR 97227
https://microcosmpublishing.com/catalog/zines/13114
Price: $6.99 US / Size: 7" x 8.5" / Pages: 48

So I legit yelped with glee when this rad little book appeared in my review stack this time. I'm kind of a science nerd, and I'll admit that some of my quarantine self-soothing has involved doing a little bit of coloring since my pandemic-brain has made it a little more challenging to focus on a lot of long-form reading. (I did, however, make it through David Chang's new memoir, *Eat a Peach*, which I was particularly stoked to be able to order through the mighty and lovely Book Moon, one town over from my own.)

From the back cover: "Lesbian lizards, gay orgies of manatees, polyamorous oystercatchers, trans clownfish, bisexual red deer, and masturbating bonobos! This coloring book celebrates the diversity of animals and the way our beautiful queer communities exist far beyond the realms of human culture. So many of us grew up with wildlife programs and school biology classes that never once mention these natural aspects of life on Earth. It was all 'male meets female, seduces her with his bright feathers or funky dance and they very quickly mate.' The implication has always been that the whole point of life is to make little baby animals and there was nothing in the great natural world that might challenge the cis-het norms of biologists. This entertaining and educational resource, created by trans woman and ecologist Otter Lieffe, and richly illustrated by Anja Van Geert, liberates this knowledge and helps free us all to express our true selves." This book does NOT disappoint; the illustrations are amazing and the actual content is much more illuminating than this back-cover-blurb suggests.

There's an awful lot of coloring-books-for-adults content out there, but this one's a must-read – it's hilarious and nerdy and awesome.

**ESSENTIAL OILS TO DESTROY THE PATRIARCHY: REMEDIES FORMULATED FOR MODERN WOMEN (& 1,000-YEAR-OLD WITCHES)**

By Eryn Nicole O'Neal
Available through Microcosm Publishing:
Microcosm Publishing,
2752 N Williams Ave, Portland, OR 97227
https://microcosmpublishing.com/catalog/zines/11450
Price: $4.99 US / Size: 4.25" x 5.5" / Pages: 38

I super enjoyed reading this zine. I enjoy zines where I learn something new and it's shared in a way that's interesting and factual but also really gets the context. This zine absolutely gets it, and it's worth reading especially if either of these subjects are of interest. It works as a recipe book/how-to while also delivering some delightfully scathing social commentary. I don't know a ton about essential oils, but ugh, argh, I'm well acquainted with the patriarchy. The layout of this little book is crisp and easy to follow (though the type is on the smaller side, so be aware if that's something that will affect your reading experience), and you can see pictures of the cover (which is particularly lovely) on the website. The book includes recipes for different blends along with how to use them (topically vs. diffusing them, for example), with an extra hilarious heaping of sarcasm (seriously, the level of snark in this book is top-notch, and I'm legit here for all of it). The names of the blends are a particular delight. Don't miss getting a copy of this one.

**YOU ARE A GREAT AND POWERFUL WIZARD: SELF-CARE MAGIC FOR MODERN MORTALS**

Available from Microcosm:
Microcosm Publishing,
2752 N Williams Ave, Portland, OR 97227
https://microcosmpublishing.com/catalog/books/7935
Written by Sage Liskey / Illustrated by Barbara Counsi
Price: $19.95US / Size: 5" x 7" (hardcover book, full color) / Pages: 288

Listen, no matter your feelings on the subject matter, this book is exquisite. The cover and endpapers are incredibly beautiful, and the internal composition and fonts are really compelling. The content is fascinating (there's also a glossary of terms and an extensive bibliography (again, some of the book is in very small type), but my first impression was basically, holy wow, this book is gorgeous. As I dove in a bit to the book, a lot of what I was reading was about good self-care and different strategies for coping and surviving. It's kind of a personal reference guide, and each chapter ends with some good questions for self-reflection. The introduction gets into more detail, explaining the book's structure and how to use it, but it's also a great guide for one's own self-reflection and thinking (even if you aren't as sure about the magic framework or the language used in the book, it's important content for folks to think about and you can apply it outside of the magic context.)

From the back cover: "Your words and actions have tremendous power. Learn how to harness that power to change your life and make the world a better place with this modern spell book – regardless of your religion or spiritual leanings. Contemporary life is confusing and it's easy to feel out of control. In this smart, secular witchcraft manual, Sage Liskey shows you how to get in touch with the mental, emotional, and physical aspects needed for spell casting. Chapters include guidance on finding your highest form, understanding your wizarding type, controlling your magic, overcoming roadblocks to your power such as depression and trauma, finding love or your ideal career, working with magical objects facing a crisis, and community spell work. Once you've fully tapped into your magical powers, you can use them to effect positive change in yourself and those around you."

I actually really enjoyed reading this book and thinking about many of the points raised within it. It's a great spark for doing exactly the kind of deep-dive thinking the introduction outlines, and I'm glad I got the chance to engage with it – it isn't a book I would have bought for myself to read, but I've enjoyed the time I've spent with it. Worth checking out.

## carlos palacios

**Adolph-Kolping Str 5**
**Dietzenbach- 63128 Germany**
**recontrapunk@hotmail.com**
**entesanomicos.com**

**TUFF: SPECIAL COLLECTIONS VOLUME I**
Robert Newsome
231 Rhodes Dr., Athens, GA 30606
secondperiod@gmail.com
theatomicelbow.bigcartel.com
Price: $5 plus shipping / Trades: yes
Size: 5.5" x 8.5" / Pages: 40

This publication is all about the hair-metal band Tuff. I wasn't familiar with them, so for the sake of this review, and to better understand what the editor talks about, I gave them a listen. To be honest, they sound pretty rad, and now I can better understand why this guy wanted to make a zine about this band. **TUFF** is primarily a photozine, containing information about each photo. It works really well as a rock document, delivering the energy of a good live show while also offering a glimpse behind the scenes. An interesting, clearly designed read.

**PONDER POND #6**
DB Pedlar or A.S. Cruz
25727 Cherry Hill Rd.,
Cambridge Springs, PA 16403
Price: Free for the asking / Trades: Yes
Size: 5.5" x 8.5" / Pages: 20

Questions, questions, and more questions – and, if you are lucky, finding answers to those questions – are the central theme of this zine. Not only does the author ponder these matters, he makes the zine interactive by encouraging readers to submit their own questions. It was nice to read a question that I also had on my own mind. With its friendly tone, **PONDER POND** prompts readers to learn more by asking questions.

**OBSESSED WITH BASS: THE ESSENTIAL HISTORY OF MIAMI BASS 1985-1993**
Aaron Nemec
Microcosm Publishing,
2752 N Williams Ave, Portland, OR 97227
https://microcosmpublishing.com/catalog/zines/11983
Price: $4.95 US / Size: 5.5 x 8.5" / Pages: 30

Having been into underground music since 1996, I am always very interested to read/see/hear how scenes were created, their sounds, and influences. This zine documents Miami's bass/funk/rap scene in the mid-'80s. Articles by and about the people who helped shape this scene provide a lot of facts and inside information, making for some interesting reading. To be sure, I am listening to the albums and artists featured here as I write this review, and I love them!

**RAZORCAKE # 112**
Razorcake
PO Box 42129, Los Angeles,CA 90042
razorcake.org
Price: $3 / Size: 8.5 x 11 / Pages: 112

It is always a pleasure to read this mag, especially when printed punk zines have become a very rare species. Every time I pick up an issue of **RAZORCAKE**, I am glad to read that there are still great bands, projects, zinesters, and artists that are tending the underground flame (as usual, #112 offers a lot to read about hxcpunk underground counterculture). You can do your part by buying or subscribing to this magazine.

**RAZORCAKE # 113**
Razorcake
PO Box 42129,Los Angeles,CA 90042
razorcake.org
Price: $3 / Size: 8.5 x 11 / Pages: 112

The pages of this labor of love for hxcpunk are always packed with columns, reviews, comics, interviews, fliers, and more. With every issue, **RAZORCAKE** delivers high-quality content and information about this influential subculture. The magazine embodies the mantra "think globally, act locally" through its support for both local and international scenes, contextualizing them as parts of a greater whole.

**PO Box A1412, Sydney South NSW 1235, Australia**
**danhelen@idx.com.au**
**bettypaginated.blogspot.com**

*The days go on and on...they don't end. – Travis Bickle*

**FANTASTIC ADVENTURES**
David McDonald (editor)
hiberniabook@eircom.net
https://www.facebook.com/HiberniaComics
Price: $15/£10.49
Size: 8.3" x 11.7" (A4) / Pages: 92

This very geeky magazine focuses mainly on various British comics that never got off the ground for one reason or another (usually financial). If you grew up in the 1970s, reading the British weekly comics (like I did) such as *2000AD, Battle Picture Weekly, Action*, and *Tiger* – or even got into the hipper, more mature titles of the late-'80s, such as *Crisis* and *Deadline* – then you'll drool over this high-quality zine packed with features and artwork on such "lost" titles as *Zarjaz!, Eureka, Glory Glory, Renga!*, and more. Elsewhere, the magazine reprints a 1981 interview with British juvenile humour comic artist Robert Nixon (who drew such strips as "Frankie Stein" and "Kid Kong"), and talks to just about everyone involved with the creatively inventive but poor-selling adult title *Revolver*. Really, I can't fault **FANTASTIC ADVENTURES** one bit, other than for the type's tiny point size. As a guy in his 50s with failing eyesight, I found it nearly impossible to read the articles without a strong overhead light.

**JOURNEY PLANET #50**
James Bacon, Michael Carroll, Christopher J. Garcia, Paul Trimble (editors)
journeyplanet@gmail.com or
jamesbacon74@email.com
www.efanzines.com or
www.journeyplanet.weebly.com
Price: FREE / Size: 8.3" x 11.7" (A4) / Pages: 197

This British-based e-zine has been publishing insightful, well-researched issues on various eclectic topics since 2007. Subjects tackled range from US and UK subways and *Dune* to all things Australia and 1950s comic space hero Dan Dare. I downloaded NO. 50 because it celebrated the 45th anniversary of the release of the first issue of the popular British boys' weekly anthology *Battle Picture Weekly*. I read this title religiously for 3-4 years as a child, before moving onto the more sophisticated weeklies like *2000AD* and, later, the American monthlies from Marvel and DC. I loved the ongoing strips in *Battle*, both for their artwork and their rollicking storylines. Of course, it being English and mainstream and the 1970s, *Battle* generally depicted square-jawed Allied heroes beating up "the Krauts" or "the Japs". It was horribly un-PC, but typical of the era. That said, amidst the xenophobia and gleeful (but child-friendly) warmongering, there were things to admire about *Battle*. It fostered some great creative talent over its 13-year run, like Spanish artist Carlos Ezquerra and English writer Gerry Finley-Day. It was also home to one of the most revered and strikingly anti-war serials ever produced, *Charley's War*, by Pat Mills and Joe Colquhoun. Maybe because it was set during World War I – and even *Battle* acknowledged that THAT particular conflict was utterly STUPID – the strip was a grim, at-times shocking examination of the horrors of trench warfare seen through the innocent eyes of 16-year-old army recruit Charley Bourne. If you like in-depth examinations on niche subjects, then **JOURNEY PLANET** is for you – each issue is loaded with stacks of articles, interviews, and tons of great artwork.

**THE TYPO KING #62.5**
Robert Jennings,
29 Whiting Rd,
Oxford, MA, 01540-2035, USA
fabficbks@aol.com
Price: Email for price details
Size: 8.3" x 11.7" (A4) / Pages: 8

This publication "of intensely personal comment and opinion" is meant to be bimonthly, but I haven't received any further issues since July, so who really knows? Robert is getting on in years, and I hope he's not been affected by "the plague," as he calls it. This issue looks at his year so far coping with the COVID-19 crisis, plus his views on the state of the comic book industry in 2020 and his attempts to shed some of his huge dime novel collection on eBay. Robert has a friendly, conversational writing style.

**FADEAWAY #64**

Robert Jennings,
29 Whiting Rd,
Oxford, MA, 01540-2035, USA
fabficbks@aol.com
Price: LOC or print fanzine (trade),
$25 six-issue subscription
Size: 8.3" x 11.7" (A4) / Pages: 38

Robert discusses the effects of coronavirus on the comics and book industries, as well as himself (he's 77-years-old, and knows that if he catches COVID-19, then that's the end of him). It's a sobering thought that's made him want to push on and achieve as much as he can before something terrible happens to him. It was in this issue that I learned of the sad passing of Steve Stiles, an artist who migrated from the fanzine world into underground comix and later mainstream success. He provided both the front cover illo and a spot illo on page 3. This issue also features pieces from other contributors, including an overview of *The Fly* series of films. Robert also has lengthy reviews on several zines and a fairly big LOC section. Overall, I really enjoyed **FADEAWAY** – I hope Robert survives COVID-19 and keeps producing issues for many years to come. Actually, I extend that hope to everyone around the world who makes zines.

**WRESTLING OBSERVER NEWSLETTER**

October 26, 2020
Dave Meltzer, PO Box 1228,
Campbell, CA, 95009-1228, USA
Dave@wrestlingobserver.com
http://www.f4wonline.com/
Price: Check site for subscriptions
Size: 8.3" x 11.7" (A4) / Pages: 24

Another news-packed issue examines Kota Ibushi's second consecutive victory in New Japan's *G-1 Climax* series, as well as the tragic death of 23-year-old Mexican luchador Principe Aereo from a brain aneurysm during a match. There are also reports on how COVID-19 is affecting various promotions around the world. For up-to-the-minute news on all things wrestling and MMA related, you should not miss Dave's intelligent, thorough weekly report.

**HYPNO VIDEO #14**

Dr Kobb
Kobb Labs, PO Box 30231,
Pensacola, FL, 32503, USA
Price: Trade only
Size: 5.8" x 8.3" (A5) / Pages: 12

This special "Naughty Nurses" issue features Kobb reviewing a bunch of kinky, hospital-related flicks, including *The Student Nurses* (1970), *Nurse Sherri* (1978), *The Sensuous Nurse* (1975), and *Young Doctors in Love* (1982). Good, clean, trashy fun.

**BIBLIO-CURIOSA #9**

Chris Mikul, PO Box K546,
Haymarket, NSW, 1240, AUSTRALIA
chris.mikul88@gmail.com
Price: AUD$5 (Australia)/email for prices (overseas)
Size: 8.3" x 11.7" (A5) / Pages: 56

This meatier-than-usual installment is "The Autobiographies and Memoirs Issue", with Chris examining some more of the most obscure books you've never heard of. I particularly enjoyed the articles on EW Martell's *Some Bods Move On*, a fantastic book about a very ordinary man; G. Gordon

Liddy's terrifying memoir *Will* (I read this in the mid-'80s, and it left an indelible mark on my brain); and the extraordinary *Crook Frightfulness*, by A. Victim. I've met someone who claimed she was a Targeted Individual, and her experiences were very similar to that of the lattermost author; I'd consider A. Victim's paranoid memoir from 1936 as a very early example of a TI. Chris has again excelled in his book selection and research on the various writers. His zines never disappoint me.

**CUL-DE-SAC #8**



Liz Mason and Julie Halpern
P.O. Box 477553, Chicago, IL 60647
caboosezine@gmail.com,
julie@juliehalpern.com
lizmasonisawesome.com, juliehalpern.com
Price: $4 US / Trades: Unknown
Size: 8.5" x 5.5" / Pages: 32

For me, perzines provide a certain sense of comfort in times of trouble. Reading about other people's lives, be they presented in daily comics or remembrances of younger days, always gives me a sense of connection, even if the artists and authors typically would be considered the Other (we are all connected in one way or another, though).

One of my favorite per-zines is Liz Mason and Julie Halpren's **CUL-DE-SAC**. There's heart and humor and authenticity in their storytelling, and for 20 or 30 minutes, I get to escape the present and lose myself in their pasts.

Issue #8 of **CUL-DE-SAC** is subtitled "Past Lives" and contains essays about the closing of Toys R Us and the death of The Bagel Restaurant and Deli in Skokie, Illinois. Liz writes about dumping a guy because he didn't like *The Matrix*, and Julie takes us on a tour of a *Supernatural* ("the TV show, not like ghosts and shit") convention. (By the way, I have never seen an episode, but my 86-year-old mother-in-law recently discovered it, and she loves it.) Liz reprints a version of an essay she wrote about the seminal '80s dance movie *Girls Just Want to Have Fun*, and unfortunately, the only thing I took away from the piece was the brief mention that Cyndi Lauper's song of the same title, which doesn't appear in the movie, was actually a cover. That threw my whole teenaged existence into question. I was so blown away, I now tell everyone I meet that fact, whether they care or not. Julie ends the zine with a tale that may make you hate humanity less, which is sorely needed these days.

Great writing and great production value for only four bucks? These ladies are doing God's work.

**SLUTCAKE #9 (JULY 2020)**
Jolie Ruin
riotgrrrlpress.etsy.com
mrsnoggle@yahoo.com
riotgrrrlpress.etsy.com
Price: $2 US / Trades: Unknown
Size: 8.5" x 5.5" / Pages: 32

I'm a big fan of Jolie Ruin's collages. She finds beauty and unity in the chaotic, using a medium that I couldn't begin to replicate. I was excited to see a new issue of **SLUTCAKE** was available, so I snagged a copy.

In this issue, subtitled "Teenage", Julie has collected essays and art about the pain and joy of growing up. Some entries are short pieces and poems, while some are longer, like attending the 2000 Vans Warped Tour. There are articles on friendship, finding love in a car, and being used by men. There are also a couple of pages of pictures of the notebooks Jolie collaged when she was in her late-teens.

The writing is as raw and heartfelt as the presentation, and though most of the remembrances are from artists who experienced their teenaged lives a few years after my own, the stories and sentiments are frighteningly familiar.

**NO SCENE ZINE #3**
B-Side, JulyTimesSheets, and Spacebar
editor@noscenezine.com
www.noscenezine.com
Price: $4 US / Trades: Unknown
Size: 8.5" x 5.5" / Pages: 14

Despite never having heard of **NO SCENE ZINE**, I nevertheless tossed a copy in my cart because of the black and white drawing of a cartoon cat in a mask and a five-piece bathing suit, holding a full-color can of Lime-A-Rita while lying on a dead fish floaty in the water. Yeah. I had to know more about this.

Issue #3 is about summer flings. (From their website, it looks like issue #1 was about cats and issue #2 was about Showbiz Pizza Palace, which spun off from Chuck E. Cheese.) From the intro: "This issue is dedicated to those hobbies, passions, summer moments of brilliance or obsession that were all but forgotten by Thanksgiving in hopes that you'll rekindle that childhood curiosity."

There's a piece on rollerblading in 1994, how to find your summer fling, and summering in a motor home. They also provide a Spotify summer playlist and a recipe for making Lime-A-Rita pops.

I don't know who the authors (author?) are, but from this full-color zine printed on thick, glossy paper, I'm guessing one or more are graphic designers. All three issues of the zine are on their website, so you can get a feel for their sensibilities, though I recommend purchasing a handheld version of this fun publication.

**HAPPY TAPIR: ON THE MAKE AT THE DRAKE #6**
Johnny Masiulewicz
happytapir1@gmail.com
www.artcityjax.com
Price: $3 US / Trades: Inquire
Size: 8.5" x 5.5" / Pages: 40

Based on a review in issue 47 of **XEROGRAPHY DEBT** (oh yeah, I read every word you punks write), I tracked down a copy of **HAPPY TAPIR #5**. When it arrived, I placed it in my To-Be-Read pile, where it sits untouched to this day.

But that didn't stop me from ordering **HAPPY TAPIR #6**, which has become one of my favorite reads this year. Subtitled "On the Make at the Drake", this issue contains essays from when Johnny worked as a "BellMan" at the Drake Hotel in Chicago. The Drake just celebrated its 100th birthday, and Johnny worked there for three years when it turned 70.

I love this zine. You may or may not know, but workplace tales are my jam, and **ON THE MAKE AT THE DRAKE** satisfies all of my terrible job fantasies. Johnny gives us engrossing vignettes about the guests and his co-workers. There's even a piece on dissing Vanna White and one about getting screwed by Bill Cosby.

It's a fun read, made even better because of my own days of hospitality service – it reminded me of the year I worked at the front desk of a shitty Best Western in Tuscaloosa, Alabama, that was owned by an obese New Jerseyan who was rumored to be a part of the mob. Man, do I have stories.

**NEXT LEVEL ALLY: HOW TO SUPPORT YOUR QUEER AND TRANSGENDER FRIENDS**
Eli Sachse (Microcosm)
2752 N Williams Ave., Portland, OR 97227
https://microcosmpublishing.com/catalog/zines/13473
Price: $4.95 US / Trades: No
Size: 8.5" x 5.5" / Pages: 38

Robin and I got married in a two-stoplight town in the middle of rural Alabama. Though everyone who knew Robin figured she wanted to recite her wedding vows barefoot on the beach, she always wanted to get married in the Baptist church she grew up in. (That doesn't mean the hippie vibe didn't permeate the entire ceremony, from the music to the vows.)

It was a small service, attended by family and close friends, and afterward, we had a PFLAG meeting before adjourning for cake and birdseed throwing.

I kid about the PFLAG meeting (but not about the birdseed), but it's a joke that's been bandied around these past thirty years. There were more gays in the pews of that staid Southern church than on a typical Sunday (well, more out gays, at least).

Robin and I are that couple. Everyone came out to us in college, and through all of our travels, we've been the community for those who feel like outsiders in their own homes and skin. And yet, my younger self would have appreciated Eli Sachse's terrific guide, **NEXT LEVEL ALLY: HOW TO SUPPORT YOUR QUEER AND TRANSGENDER FRIENDS** (especially before I made an off-handed and tasteless joke to a friend's new boyfriend, now husband; it happened 25 years ago, and though he probably doesn't hold it against me, it still stings when I think about it). Even now, as we've passed our openness to our children, who are forceful allies, I found some points in Sachse's pamphlet to appreciate, and I've passed it along to the next generation.

**NEXT LEVEL ALLY** is about understanding your friends and being a vocal advocate. It should be given away to high school counselors and left out as free grabs in every friendly bookstore.

**IT'S GOING TO BE ANARCHY: ANARCHIST ANALYSIS OF THE CORONAVIRUS PANDEMIC**
Jim Donaghey (Microcosm)
2752 N Williams Ave., Portland, OR 97227
https://microcosmpublishing.com/catalog/zines/13298
Price: $4.95 US / Trades: No
Size: 4.25" x 5.5" / Pages: 46

There are always one or two zines in my packet from Davida that I will pass over, and after thumbing through Jim Donaghey's pocket-sized **IT'S GOING TO BE ANARCHY** from Microcosm, I figured this would be one such publication.

Written between late-March and early-April 2020 (and appearing first on his blog, I believe), this is a look at the "wide range of anarchist responses to the coronavirus/Covid-19 pandemic."

My first instinct was, "No, thanks." Who wants to relive the early moments of this nightmare? But I was a little curious about what Jim was espousing, so I gave it a chance.

Unfortunately, like most thick, pseudo-scholarly pieces written what seems like 47 years ago, this does not hold up.

The British point of view is interesting (though the section on work came off as a little naïve), but here's the thing: On this side of the pond, we are being led by an anarchist. Our life isn't going to be anarchy, it has been for the last four years, so I can't take this line of thought seriously anymore.

With everything that has happened since April – and I mean everything – I consider Jim's publication quaint – something historians may be interested in when the next hundred-year pandemic hits.

The cover is cool, though.

**GOING ON TOUR: PERFECT MIX TAPE SEGUE #4**

Joe Biel (Microcosm)
2752 N Williams Ave., Portland, OR 97227
https://microcosmpublishing.com/catalog/zines/1359
Price: $4.95 US / Trades: No
Size: 7" x 4.25" / Pages: 62

I'm not sure, but I think this is a reprint of **PERFECT MIX TAPE SEGUE #4** with a new introduction and postscript. But whatever form it first appeared in, Joe Biel's **GOING ON TOUR**, the zine tour-based zine about Cocoon: The Road Trip, is a fascinating read.

It's 2004, and Joe, armed with his new documentary, *$100 & a T-Shirt*, along with Nicole J Georges (**INVINCIBLE SUMMER**), Dave Roche (**ON SUBBING**), and Jack Saturn (**WE AIN'T GOT NO CAR**) pile into a truck and head for Olympia, Washington, for their first stop in a tour around the states.

I admire Joe and friends for going on an adventure that scares the crap out of me. This is one of those let-me-live-vicariously-through-you reads, and I did. I loved the hand-drawn maps and the photos. The stories were wonderful, and I liked the bit about where everyone was now. The whole experience made me anxious, and I enjoyed it.

**BEHIND THE ZINES #10 (JULY 2020)**

Billy McCall
1600 Coal Ave., SE,
Albuquerque, NM 87106 **[new address]**
iknowbilly@gmail.com
iknowbilly.etsy.com
Price: $3 US / Trades: Maybe
Size: 8.5" x 5.5" / Pages: 40

I've missed a couple of issues of Billy's zine about zines, **BEHIND THE ZINES**, and that's my own damn fault, but I've got a copy of issue 10 (10!), and it's just as fun and informative as the previous issues I've read.

There are some familiar (to me) zinesters and some not-so-familiar (to me) in this issue. There are a couple of articles on owning your own copier and a comic about "zinetiquette." Liz Mason writes about her adventures in zine data mining, and Gianni Simone recounts how he went from zines to magazines. Brian Polk's "Zines I Would Make if I Didn't Have to Worry about Time or Money" was delightful, and there are even back-page zine reviews.

Don't be like me: keep up with each new issue and submit something for possible inclusion in a future issue, if you haven't already.

**KER-BLOOM! ISSUE 145**
**JULY/AUGUST 2020**
Artnoose
2480 5th St., Berkeley, CA 94710
http://www.etsy.com/shop/artnoose?ref=pr_shop_more
Price: $3 US / Size: 4.25"x5.5" / Pages: 12

What I like about Artnoose's **KER-BLOOM!** is that I can go months or years without coming across a copy, but when I do, like an old friend, I'm always excited to see it. This little letterpress publication never fails to delight, and issue 145 is no exception. I picked it up because of the wood-cut picture of a green fire-breathing dragon on the cover. It's about the first time Artnoose almost played Dungeons & Dragons (as introduced in a great non-sequitur opening). It's a short remembrance about creating characters for a campaign, including a green dragon. My only complaint is that the zine ended just as the adventure was starting.

**FOUR ANECDOTES ABOUT DAVID BOWIE FROM MY OWN LIFE**
Joseph Carlough
joseph@displacedsnail.com
www.displacedsnail.com
Price: $3 US / Size: 5.5" x 3.5" / Pages: 11

This was one of those zines that I picked up purely because of the title. David Bowie never makes a personal appearance in Joseph's four short anecdotes, but his presence in Joseph's life looms large. It's a sweet zine about friendship, family, sexuality, and Halloween costumes. It's well-written, and I thoroughly enjoyed it.

**POSER FAIL: A PUNK GAME**
Bryan
2220 16th Ave South,
Minneapolis, MN 55404
poserfail@riseup.net
Price: $4 US / Trades: Only for games
Size: 8.5" x 5.5" / Pages: 38

I am not a poser. I can type that with confidence, not because I fit in, but because it's obvious I don't – anywhere. And if you have to ask, I will straight up tell you I do not belong. Growing up, I was the kid that flittered around the outskirts of all groups. Liked by many – Belong to none. That was my motto. I was Ferris without the coolness or confidence. So **POSER FAIL: A PUNK GAME** is not for me. But I would love to hang out with you guys and watch it being played.

The premise is simple: "Amongst every crew of true life punks, there is at least one poser pretending to be one of you." The object of the game is to suss out the punk poser. (Clue #1 I'm not a punk: Using the term "suss out.")

There is one page of instructions and 36 pages of chits you are supposed to cut out and pass around. At the start of the round, all players receive cards showing the same location, like a bike coop, or punk house, or tree sit, except for one player gets the "poser" card. And then everyone starts asking questions to give clues to where you are, and the poser has to figure out the location until someone discovers the poser.

If you've got a punk posse (is that a thing?), give the game a try. If not, the game pieces were fun to read.

**WORTH A WASHINGTON! VOLUME 3, #6 (ISSUE 25), JUNE 2020**
Markell Raphaelson West
115 Irving Street, Laurel, M 2070-450315
markellorhighwater@gmail.com
Price: $1 US, or anything with a Washington on it (but see review) / Trades: Free by email
Size: 8.5" x 11" / Pages: 10

**WORTH A WASHINGTON!** is a writer's workshop community zine that's free to contributors (of which there were 13 for this issue) and free by email to anyone.

Markell West is the zine's compiler and editor, and the zine contains an Open Forum, where you can write about anything, followed by writing prompts and the responses they elicit from the "Cast of Contributors". Each prompt has a number beside it, designating where it falls in the history of this zine (it looks like they are up to 290 prompts, including those for July 2020, but you can respond to earlier prompts, I believe). It's a confusing, scattershot setup, but the prompts and responses are fun to read. And I liked the list of words on the front page that Markell has had to add to her spellcheck dictionary.

By the way, in a recent letter from Markell, I found out that the new title of the zine is **JUST A JEFFERSON!** (although she's still deciding on the exclamation point), and a copy will cost you a $2.00 bill (or maybe she was just being funny).

**DITHERING DOODLES #131, #132**
Steven Anderson
259E 700 S. Salt Lake City, UT 84111
premiumdelux@hotmail.com
Price: $2 US / Trades: Inquire
Size: 5.5" x 8.5" / Pages: 10, 10

In issue 131, Steven celebrates his return to work at the Grand America Hotel (in Salt Lake City) after a six-month COVID-19 vacation without pay. (During that layoff, he worked on over a dozen **DITHERING DOODLES** and got a "Basket Bawl Tummy.") Now, he's back to vacuuming the lobby and cleaning the public areas and listening to "muzik" from the era of "Puttin' on the Ritz". And there are tweakers in the park. And he's got a bad tooth.

In issue 132, Steven forgets to put out the garbage, draws more about the Grand America Hotel, and adds some caricatures about the 1961 cult movie *Carnival of Souls*. And there are more "dumb dumb commix strips." And lots of Corona viruses.

But you don't come to **DITHERING DOODLES** to catch up on Steven's life – you come for the doodles and the rebuses. It's a few minutes of charming inanity that gives you a break from all the insanity.

**PO Box 347, Glen Arm, MD 21057**
**www.leekinginc.com**
**davida@leekinginc.com**

**I'VE WORN ALL THE SHIRTS IN THE DRAWER: 64 DAYS OF T-SHIRTS DURING COVID-19**
PO Box 877, Lansdowne, PA 19050
syndprod@gmail.com
syndprod.etsy.com
Price: $5 US / Trades: Inquire
Size: 4.25" x 5.5" / Pages: 68

**GOT A BOX FULL OF T-SHIRTS: SEQUEL TO I'VE WORN ALL THE SHIRTS IN THE DRAWER**
Syndicate Product HQ
Aj Michel
PO Box 877, Lansdowne, PA 19050
Price: $3 US / Trades: Inquire
Size: 4.25" x 5.5" / Pages: 20

I needed these zines. **I'VE WORN ALL THE SHIRTS IN THE DRAWER** in particular. The early days of the quarantine were psychological chaos. We were "in this together", but isolated. We were under threat, but the days were often beautiful. Aj found a way to document those days by wearing each of the t-shirts in her drawer. Each day comes with an image of the shirt and what was going on internally and externally. I'm at a loss to explain how perfect this zine is at documenting a place and time in history in a very personal way. It is about the past (t-shirts), present (pandemic), and future (so much anxiety). It also helped me connect with someone else feeling so many of the same feelings. This is the zine I needed to help process some of my own thoughts and feelings. Highly recommended.

**GOT A BOX FULL OF T-SHIRTS** is a much shorter sequel and goes through a box of t-shirts. It also provides additional closure about the project.

**ZINES BY BILLY ROBERTS/BILLY MCCALL**
1600 Coal Ave., SE, Albuquerque, NM 87106
[new address]
iknowbilly@gmail.com
iknowbilly.etsy.com

**THE DESERT SUN #2, #4, #6, #7, #8, #9, #10, #11, #12, #13, #14**
Price: $1 / Trades: likely
Size: 4.25" x 5.5" / Pages: 24

I'm impressed how Billy has kept up such a steady publishing schedule. I binge-read most of these and they helped me understand why I haven't been reading zines as much over the last few months. Between the pandemic and election, it was all I could do to keep going day-to-day. Zines are the realest form of media I consume. They are honest and unfiltered. And I have been shying away from that lately in favor of fiction and distraction. It has been hard enough living my own reality and living someone else's fears and anxieties was a bit more than I could handle. Zines, especially per-zines, are almost like socializing and I was finally ready to talk to people again when I sat down to catch up on my zine reading.

After an issue or two, I started to feel like I was hanging out with Billy. It felt like the lunches we would occasionally have when he lived in Baltimore. These short zines offer glimpses into Billy and Alicia's lives and thoughts. These issues cover the move back to Albuquerque, having to move to a new house, a foster dog, COVID, being furloughed, birthdays, and more. A ream of personality on one sheet of paper.

**PROOF I EXIST #30**
Price: $1 / Trades: likely
Size: 4.25" x 5.5" / Pages: 16

This issue of **PROOF I EXIST** was written in one night, while Billy was drinking wine with his partner and a friend. He starts out explaining his life and life choices. And then it is nightfall and several glasses later and he begins questioning those choices. He thinks about all the places he's lived and some of the people he has loved. He is up and down as he types away. We've all had these nights, but Billy captured the moment.

**GRASSHOPPERS ARE COMING**
Alicia H.
1600 Coal Ave., SE, Albuquerque, NM 87106
iknowbilly@gmail.com
iknowbilly.etsy.com
Price: $1 / Trades: likely
Size: 4.25" x 5.5" / Pages: 24

Billy's partner, Alicia, created her first zine this summer. While in the midst of the pandemic, she read a book about the plague of locusts that covered the Midwest in the late-1800s. She is utterly horrified by the descriptions of millions upon millions of grasshoppers descending upon the land. I was also interested to learn that the locust effectively disappeared. My one criticism is that I would like to have seen more of Alicia's writing in the issue.

**THE KEN CHRONICLES #55, #56**
**SQUIRRELS ATE MY APPLES #57**

Ken Bausert
2140 Erma Drive,
East Meadow, NY 11554-1120
passscribe@aol.com
thekenbausertchronicles.blogspot.com
Price: $3.50 US, Canada, Mexico / $4 Rest of World; 4 issue subscription $10 US
Trades: Fair trades or a letter of comment
Size: 5.5" x 8.5" / Pages: 24

Ken has decided to rename his long-running zine **SQUIRRELS ATE MY APPLES**. The only thing that has changed is the name. It is still 100% Ken. **#55** was produced while Ken was staying put in Florida, while COVID raged in NY. It deviates from his usual format, but it still the usual mix of what Ken has been doing, reading, thinking about, and fixing. Speaking of fixing things, can I suggest more installments of Kenning-it®? Ken can fix about anything and often explains what was broken and that he fixed it. Sometimes he includes the how, but not always. What about a column that explains some basic fix-it tips? Or even explaining how things work? His days as a mechanic and homeowner make him an expert in many things that baffle laypeople.

By the time it was safe for him to go home, Florida had become a hot spot. He talks about coming home and you can see how the last several months and losing another friend are bothering him. He sets about working on one of his bucket list items – to read all of his Carl Banks comics.

Many people staying at home are binge-watching TV, but Ken being Ken, he hired someone to strip his wallpaper and painted the walls himself. There is a bit more reading and watching in **#57**, but he still had time to get in some family visits before the second wave hit.

**DO NOT PET: A SERVICE DOG'S GRAPHIC TAIL**

Joe Biel with Caroline Spark, PhD
Available from Microcosm Publishing (https://microcosmpublishing.com/catalog/zines/9453)
Price: $4.95 / $6.49 CAN / Trades: No
Size: 10.125" x 6.625" / Pages: 32

This one hurt a bit. I had known Ruby, Joe Biel's service dog, for many years. In fact, it was one of my photos that helped add to her book-world celebrity. Every time I saw her, she was working, so despite my desire to make friends all I could do was smile at her and bring her cookies. She passed away the day her story came back from the printer.

**DO NOT PET** is a comic geared toward all ages and is not just Ruby's story, but the history of service dogs. Dogs have worked with and for humans on battlefields, as seeing eye dogs, and assisting in investigations. Dogs can also detect medical issues in people, including seizures, allergies, and blood sugar issues.

Joe has several medical issues, one of which is plummeting glucose levels that cause him to pass out. It seemed the path to getting a medical service dog would be difficult, but trainer he chose to work with thought it might be possible to find a rescue dog. She said it might take some time. The next day, Ruby appears in the story. She begins her training to become Joe's service dog.

**DWAN #83: AUGUST 2020**
**DVAN ECHINODERM SPCIAL (83) NOT QUITE A ZINE, NOT QUITE A LETTER, NOT QUITE PUBLIC(ATION)**

Donny Smith
dwanzine@gmail.com
Price: secret handshake (or maybe an email) Trades: Yes / Size: 8.5" x 11" / Pages: 35

The first 30 pages of this issue slip and slide through languages, time, and religions. Potatoes and sea urchins nuzzle against each other. Old words and images crash into new eyes and interpretations. It is quite dizzying. At times, it feels like a magpie's collection. And then on page 31, Donny appears. There is something about pandemic-time (era?) writing that feels more honest and raw. "The Therapist is always trying to fix things, but I don't think all things can be fixed. At least not without breaking other things." Those last five pages have been echoing in my brain for a few days.

**CUL-DE-SAC #8: PAST LIVES**

Liz Mason
PO Box 477553, Chicago, IL 60647
caboosezine@gmail.com
Lizmasonisawesome.com
LizMasonZines.etsy.com
Julie@juliehalpern.com
Juliehalpern.com
Available from Quimby's (quimbys.com) and Antiquated Future (antiquatedfuture.com)
Price: $4 US / Trade: Inquire
Size: 5.5" x 8.5" / Pages: 36

I love it when Julie and Liz get together and geek-out. This is something of a personal nostalgia trip. They eulogize The Bagel Restaurant and Deli where Julie, Liz, and their friends spent their formative years. I can't imagine having friends from grade school, so it was a curious voyeur's view to watch them move back and forth in time and into imagined and real futures. Julie also bemoans the loss of Toys R Us and what it meant to her as a kid. I totally got Liz breaking up with someone because they didn't like *The Matrix* (I once broke up with someone because he wouldn't understand why I carted an orphaned opossum around in my bra for several days. I probably didn't even explain why.) My favorite article was Julie's essay on going to *Supernatural* conventions. A window into different subcultures is everything I love about zines.

**CHITTERING MADNESS #2**

Ryan Mishap
PO Box 5841, Eugene, OR 97405
mishapzine@yahoo.com
Price: $3 US? / Trades: Inquire
Size: 5.5" x 8.5" / Pages: 48

Thanks to COVID-19, Ryan sent me the PDF version, which means I got to see the places he visited in search of birds in color. Most of you know how much I love animals and natural places, so it should come as no surprise that I think **CHITTERING MADNESS** is an absolute delight. This issue is almost more of a travel zine, but each destination offers birds that we, the readers, never get to see. At first, I was a bit frustrated by this, but then I realized the genius in this approach. Ryan is trying to entice people off their couches and phones and to pay attention to nature. Recommended.

**FAT BLACK GIRL IN A WHEELCHAIR #2 "PLAGUE DIARY"**

Bloody Mary's Cool Sister aka Miss Fran
marybld@aol.com
www.blurb.com/bookstore

$12.50 US via blurb.com; free as a PDF via email / Trades: yes
Size: 8.5" × 11" / Pages: 48

It dawns on me that many of the zines I've read document how introverts are surviving 2020. This issue is no exception. Well-edited and well-produced with some color pages, Fran talks about her and her family are holding up. Many of the problems she wrote about in her last issue – her health and employment – are at least somewhat settled. She's figured out how to manage and writing is part of it. Within the issue are there are also short works of fiction and poems.

This one section stuck me and it has become something I think about all the time, "Always give yourself something to anticipate, no matter how simple or inane. Joni Mitchell's new album is coming out next week. Tomorrow I'll try making that bean soup. Sometimes it's the little things that keep you sane. And if you're prone to depression, it will also keep you alive."

**DERRY GIRLS: A ZINE ABOUT THE GIRLS (AND THE WEE ENGLISH FELLA)**
Rebecca McCormick
5 Holdroyd's Yard,
Dodworth, Barnsley, S75 3NB, UK
clumsykisses@gmail.com
https://www.etsy.com/shop/clumsykisses
Price: $7 (included shipping) / Trades: Unknown / Size: 5.75" x8.75" / Pages: 48

I was online looking for *Derry Girls* merch for my mother when I tripped across this zine. Thanks, Etsy! I love a good fanzine that overflows with the joy of the author sharing something they love. In this case, Rebecca loves *Derry Girls*. If you, like me, were hooked from the first time Michelle bursts onto screen yelling "Motherfuckers!" this zine is for you. Sláinte, Motherfucker!

**PONDER POND #8**
DB Pedlar or A.S. Cruz
25727 Cherry Hill Rd.,
Cambridge Springs, PA 16403
Price: Free for the asking / Trades: Yes
Size: 5.5" x8.5" / Pages: 20

Weird and wonderful discussions that border on the hallucinatory at times. At heart, DB and A.S. put forth questions and discuss life, the universe and everything and anything. In this particular issue, DB mentions watching *Motherless Brooklyn*. I too enjoyed it, and when he mentioned the book and how it was a bit different, I quickly added it to my to-be-read pile. To return the favor, DB, check out Lethem's *The Feral Detective*. I enjoyed reading the crossover between Ken Bausert's zine and **PONDER POND** when it came to watching Yesterday. Lots of letters of comment and pondering. DB swerves into much deeper territory when responding to the responsibilities of anti-abortionists. This is like a zine watering hole.

**CHICAGO GETS 4 STARS: HISTORY ZINE, #1 AND #2**
Joe Mason
PO Box 477553, Chicago, IL 60647
eelobrien@gmail.com
https://www.etsy.com/shop/eelobrien
Price: $3, $1 / Trades: Inquire
Size: 5.5" x8.5" (#1), Matchbook #2 / Pages: 20

Hey, Fred, you totally need to check this one out. **CHICAGO GETS 4 STARS** is everything I want in a zine. It is well-written, the passion in Joe's voice is clear, and I learned something. In eight short essays, we learn about lesser known, often morbid, moments in Chicago's history. Did you know there was a beer riot in 1855 after Mayor Levi imposed a blue law closing taverns on

Sundays, the only day many of the working class immigrants could gather? I knew a little about PBR's history from *The Devil in the White City*, but Joe further explains the modern-day connections to Schlitz. Most chilling was the Whitechapel Club. Read the issue and you'll see what I mean. Recommended.

**ISSUE #2** was brutally clever. Order it and see what I mean.

**PECULIAR PAPER PEOPLE #7, #8, #9, #10**
Billy McKay
PO Box 542, N. Olmstead OH 44070
billytherobot@gmail.com
Billytherobot.etsy.com and billytherobot.spreadshirt.com
Price: $2 US / Trades: Yes
Size: 5.5" x 8.5" / Pages: 16, full color

Billy's work is so cheerfully morbid. I love it. His drawing style and coloring are very distinctive. His most gruesome monsters just want to be friends and his adorable creatures will happily eviscerate you. Each issue offers a main story and several small stories, and lots of doodles. The twist ending in "Lucky Steve" was amazing. In **#9**, Billy showcases art by kids, including Billy (the kid).

**SQUEAKY NUISANCE #4**
Christopher Robin
820 E. 4th Ave, Hutchinson, KS 67501
**[new address]**
junkwriter@christopherrobin.xyz
Price: not listed, send at least $5 to cover printing and mailing / Trades: Probably, inquire
Size: 5.5" x8.5" / Pages: 88 (lots of color)

There is something both loose and together about **SQUEAKY NUISANCE**. Like a song that swings out into different directions, only to come back to the melody. The song is about freedom and grief, about hope and disappointment. Sprinkled in between are collages, reviews, work by other writers, photos, and drawings. It is a per-zine in the purest form, where the reader needs to keep up with where the writer chooses to take you. Without the usual roots of family, job, hometown, or even animals, Christopher decides to move from Portland, OR, to Hutchinson, KS. Both Portland and Kansas have issues – no place is perfect, and he knows that. He travels to the Bahamas looking for a cure for MS for his partner Ramon/a. I learned that the founder of *Vice* also founded the Proud Boys; I read more on that after I finished the zine. Christopher's take on safe spaces was interesting. As a trans queer with PTSD, he is more concerned with censorship than safe spaces. Who makes them safe/unsafe? It makes for an interesting debate (I had the debate in my own head after I read his essay). I think in many cases safe spaces are created by well-meaning people who want to treat the symptoms and not the disease.

**dwanzine@gmail.com**

I spend a lot of time on BHL, the Biodiversity Heritage Library: www.biodiversitylibrary.org. And if not there, then maybe the Istanbul Sehir University Institutional Repository: earsiv.sehir.edu.tr. Much as I prefer to read from paper, getting to a real library is pretty much not possible. Bookstores are easier to get to, but not necessarily more rewarding. Luckily, Davida has sent me some zines (real zines, on paper). If you're curious about Turkish zines (PDFs anyway), you might start at Fanzine Apartmanı: fanzinapartmani.com. If you're curious about my zine, send me a message.

**ADVICE FROM HYBRID BEINGS**

Ariel Gore
arielfiona@gmail.com
literarykitchen.com
Price: $8 US / Size: 6" x 6" / Pages: 24 + color cardstock cover

Inspirationally realistic slogans matched with drawings of awkwardly magical creatures. For instance, the Fishcat recommends, "keep going deeper into your personal tide pools" (I like the idea of personal tide pools, daily filling, daily abandoned to boil out under the sun) "until you find the universal stream." Sensible, nonsensical.

**PONDER POND: A SOUP OF INTENSE THOUGHT #5**

DB Pedlar or A. S. Cruz
DB Pedlar, 25727 Cherry Hill Rd, Cambridge Springs PA 16403 USA
Price: "free for the asking" or "letters, stamps, money, reference books, trades, photos, art, etc."
Size: 5.5" x 8.5" / Pages: 20

The zine starts out asking the reader, Do you wonder what we wonder about? and goes from there. DB apparently has no feeling in his hands and feet (and other parts?). A. S. asks what that's like. DB says among other things, "I drop a lot of things," and recounts an anecdote about an Alfred E. Neuman-lookalike doctor. But of course I wonder about things like bites and infections. I guess if I had no feeling in my extremities I wouldn't be scratching my bug bites till they bled or picking at my scabs all the time. Then while discussing "the skin of our teeth," DB mentions "bare life" ("Job was doing a little show and tell as he exhibited his skin full of sores that were sagging away from the bone or splitting and revealing bone, yet he escaped with bare life ... because his gums alone were still whole ...") but doesn't go on to talk about the whole mess of philosophical bare life (not surprisingly, I guess, since later he remarks, "silly me, attempting to expect a sensible and understandable philosophy discussion." And yet they take up the question, Why knowledge? Why, when we die in the end? A question which assumes that the goal is for our knowledge to go on forever). As a conclusion (as my students say, no matter how many times I tell them not to), I miss getting DB's zines. They make me want to write him right back.

**THIS ZINE HAS ISSUES: BREAKING THE STIGMA OF MENTAL ILLNESSES**

Dave Combs
Microcosm Publishing,
2752 N Williams Ave,
Portland OR 97227 USA
microcosmpublishing.com
Price: $3.95 US
Size: 5.5" x 8.5" / Pages: 34
Focus on bipolarism. A particularly good essay, "6am Ramblings on a Sleepless Night" by Allison Leonard, a tightrope of reasoned argument over a chaos of consciousness.

**LEEKING INK #35**

Davida Gypsy Breier
PO Box 347, Glen Arm MD 21057 USA
davida@leekinginc.com
www.leekinginc.com
Price: $3 US or stamps; PDFs free / Trades: preferred / Size: 5.5" x 8.5" / Pages: 58

Eels! I thought I knew some things about them, but I didn't really. A zine of eels, but also about Davida's life. All linked in a ziney way (zinily?). The feeling of becoming at home in the ocean. The sight of fish swimming above. Eels at various ages. "I saw more eels. Some were small and almost transparent. They blended in with the greenish water and stones. Others were more opaque with a yellow hue, nearly a foot long." A little envy on my part: I don't think I've ever seen an eel in the wild (unless you count morays, which are part of the bigger Anguilliformes but not part of the Anguillidae family that she's talking about). What else? A list of things not known about eels (a surprisingly long list). Freud dissecting 400 eels trying to find eel testicles (didn't he ever analyze that?). And, non-eelly-ly, a photo of a hornworm covered in the eggs of a parasitic wasp. (Could our interests intersect in more ways?)

**STRAY BATS**

Words by Margo Lanagan, Illustrations by Kathleen Jennings
Small Beer Press, 150 Pleasant St #306, Easthampton MA 01027 USA
info@smallbeerpress.com
Price: $10 US / Size: 5.5" x 8.5" / Pages: 62 with color cover

Unfortunately, I started reading this only a day before the deadline for these reviews, so can't give much of a review. A chapbook, vignettes of magic spells. Apparently inspired by poems (a long list at the back of the book). "They might be tempted out of the hovering din to pause a moment, free from all dangers and enemies, in her red arms."

**FAT BLACK GIRL IN A WHEELCHAIR #2 "PLAGUE DIARY"**

Bloody Mary's Cool Sister aka Miss Fran
marybld@aol.com
www.blurb.com/bookstore
Price: $12.50 US via blurb.com; free as a PDF via email / Trades: yes
Size: 8.5" × 11" / Pages: 48

Again, I started reading this only a day before the deadline for these reviews. Nevertheless, I can talk about the parts that I'd already read here and there online. For instance, this COVID-y anecdote: "I was in the drugstore today to pick up the prescription I've been trying to get for the past week when this woman walks in dressed like a bag lady from *Mad Max*. She's got on a flowered shower cap for head protection, a surgical mask, a fluorescent orange rain poncho, surgical booties, goggles, the works. There's a brief pause where everyone in the store holds their breath. Is this woman a major freak out waiting to happen?" The story never ends the way I expect. This is what I love about Fran's writing. The desperation ever turning to hope. Not falsely.

**WIDOWMAKER**

Franetta McMillian
marybld@aol.com
www.amazon.com/Widowmaker-Franetta-McMillian-ebook/dp/B08MB881RL/
Price: $1 US / Size: e-book / Pages: 11

As the author told me, "New one-off for Halloween or four days before the Fall of Rome, take your pick." (If you're actually able to read this, Rome probably didn't fall very hard.) A short story that starts with a broke-down car on a country road far from anywhere and a storm on its (her) way. It doesn't end the way I expected.

**Penthouse L, 1170 Ocean Parkway, Brooklyn, NY 11230**

Since zines and the mail often go hand-in-hand, I thought I'd scribble a few words about the arrangement that's been in effect for the last 49 years – which a lot of people don't seem to know about. So set the Wayback Machine for 1971... when President Nixon took the U.S. Post Office (a government agency) and banished it to the private sector, creating USPS, the United States Postal System, a private company. The fun and games ensued almost immediately: Congress had had the right to set postal rates since George Washington's time, and they weren't about to give it up. So what Nixon did, in effect, was create a company that wouldn't be able to manage its own income. You didn't need a PhD to know what kind of trouble was going to result. We've been lucky it took half a century (and also that Congress did keep its right, or a first-class stamp would probably cost about $4 today).

These days, of course, USPS doesn't need to fumble around for excuses to cover substandard performance. They just blame it all on the coronavirus, and you're supposed to sit there and nod in agreement. Shortly before I sat down to compose these reviews, I received a letter from Minnesota on October 6. The problem was, it had been postmarked September 9. A full month from Minnesota to New York? I kept thinking they must have sent it by bicycle!

Well, as long as I can put my zines in the mail and have at least some hope of delivery before the next calendar year, I guess it isn't the end of the world. Close, maybe, but no cigar. So let's see what was in the bulky package Davida sent me (and give yourself a gold star if you guessed that I received it in time!)...

**ALTERNATIVE INCITE #1**
Joe3 (a.k.a. Joe Smith)
P.O. Box 3067, Laurel, MD 20907
joe3ofcp@gmail.com
Price: $3 US, $4 Canada/Mexico, $5 world
Size: 7x8.5" / Pages: 40

I think it's a great thing when you can start a set of reviews with something resoundingly positive. Celebrating creativity qualifies as far as I'm concerned, and that's just what we have here. Joe has started this new zine devoted to creativity. This comes from his mission statement: "[It] exists to encourage readers to follow their creative impulses and exercise their right to be bizarre, different and/or peculiar in the interest of personal satisfaction and the greater good." Had I put on my thinking cap four hours before starting to write this review, I couldn't have said it any better. Included in the inaugural issue are such thought-provoking pieces as Thoughts Provoked, Adventures in Contemporary Anachronism and What is this "New Normal" I Keep Hearing About? Hopefully, lots of people will find $3 to send Joe, get the zine, and then find themselves creatively inspired.

**CUL-DE-SAC #8: PAST LIVES**
Liz Mason, CabooseZine@gmail.com
Julie Halpern, Julie@JulieHalpern.com
P.O. Box 47753, Chicago, IL 60647
Price: $4 / Size: 5.5x8.5" / Pages: 36

So what's going on in the world of Liz and Julie? You'll have to get the zine to find out, but here's a little peek inside to whet your appetite. First, there's Eulogy for a Bagel, about the sad occurrence of a prized local restaurant/deli (and also a wonderful meeting place for zinesters!) closing its doors for good. This is followed by an R.I.P. for Toys 'R' US. But don't worry; the entire world they grew up in hasn't vanished. For instance, Julie waxes eloquent about attending a Supernatural convention – the TV show, not with ghosts or UFOs – and also observes the kindness of strangers. And while Julie's at the convention, Liz reminisces about growing up with the film *Girls Just Want to Have Fun*. It's a fun read. Fun reads are good things, and so the conclusion here should be obvious. Now... .where did you put that envelope?

**DOES THIS COUNT?**

Poetry from a Non-Poet
Don Leach
notmovingpictures@gmail.com
Price: not listed / Trades: possible!
Size: 5.5x4.5" / Pages: 12

So what happens when someone who says he isn't a poet sits down and starts composing poems? Not just any old poems, but haiku. Well, you get **DOES THIS COUNT?** I should say, as a non-poet who has had a whole notebook of poems sitting in my desk for quite a few years, that Don's efforts are pretty good. He even stays within the fairly rigid haiku syllabic limitations of 5-7-5, which a lot of people don't do (and then call their stuff haiku anyway, even though it isn't). For those of you who think that haiku has to be about cherry blossoms and ocean waves, these poems will have you thinking differently. I suppose you could call them Americanized haiku, which I, personally, would take as a compliment. Don has also mentioned that he's been suppressing the urge to make a zine devoted to sports. As a fan of that kind of thing, I'm not going to say a word to discourage him. But in the meanwhile, check this one out. And contact him for his other efforts in zinedom.

**SPEAKING OF TRAINS**

A Glossary of Modern-Day Hobo and Railroad Worker Slang
Brakeshoe
from Microcosm Publishing
2752 N. Williams Ave., Portland, OR 97227
Price: $7.95 US, $10.99 Canada
Size: 5.5x8.5"/ Pages: 70

Why do I think Davida sent this to me because she knows I'm a transit worker? Well, even if that wasn't what happened, this is still an utterly fascinating project. It begins with the original publication of rail jargon, which appeared in what was then *Railroad Man's Magazine* (1930). Everything else makes up the fifth edition, including a lot of terminology and phrases that have come into use since the original saw print. OK, OK, I work for a subway system (technically, urban mass transit) and not a railroad. Nor am I a hobo. But there are still quite a few terms here with which I'm familiar, because they cross lines. Send away for your copy ASAP, and then proceed to amaze and/or confound everyone around you with a jargon they might not understand! Communication, or, when necessary, a lack thereof, can be fun.

**LIVING FREE**

Jim Stumm
Box 29-XD, Hiler Branch, Buffalo, NY 14223
Price: $12.00/6 issues, $2.00 sample /
Trades: maybe / Size: 8.5x11" / Pages: 8

Here's a zine you can live with, literally!

Even in our great and wonderful democracy, forces are continually at work eroding the freedoms we're supposed to have. Since taking up arms against the government would be frowned upon (I may be guilty of understatement when I typed those words), knowledge is very important to have in the effort to maintain the aforementioned freedom. That's what this zine presents – the title does not imply some kind of arrangement where you don't pay rent. I have issues 165 and 166 here before me, the contents of which investigate such issues as the government taking a $108,000 house to cover a $144 tax debt, plastic in the oceans (which should be a concern if you ever eat seafood), safeguarding eminent domain reform in Georgia, victory in a New Jersey eminent domain battle for a piano tuner, and street camera surveillance. Jim accepts submissions, but you should ask for the writer's guidelines. No poetry or fiction, please. And just so you know, it's typewritten, which I don't consider to be a put-down, at all. Two thumbs up for a freedom-loving zine produced in the old-school way.

**MARKTIME #131**
Mark Strickert
P.O. Box 1171, Rialto, CA 92377
busnrail@yahoo.com
Price: $2 (also accepts trades, letters of comment) / Trades: yes
Size: 8.5 x 11" / Pages: 14

The title is kind of a double pun; the editor's name is Mark, and the zine marks the course of his life. Mark's been at it for quite a while, starting out back in the '70s in Chicago. The contents consist of what's happening in his corner of the land, including trips he's taken as well as transit notes (which Yours Truly always appreciates). Get it, read it, send in letters of comment (or, as Mark titles that section, Lettuce of Condiment) and mark some time yourself.

**JUST A JEFFERSON**
A Writer's Workshop Community Zine
Vol. 3, No. 6 (Issue 25), June 2020
Markell Raphaelson West
115 Irving St., Laurel, MD 20707-4503
markellorhighwater@gmail.com
Price: $2 / Trades: possibly
Size: 8.5 x 11" / Pages: varies; this one has 10

This used to be **WORTH A WASHINGTON!**, but Markell asks $2 for a copy... and she also happens to like the $2 bill, so a title change was probably inevitable. Don't be scared off by the subtitle. The zine does originate with a local writer's workshop, but contributions are most heartily welcomed. And you don't have to live anywhere near Laurel. Or even Maryland. I can vouch for this because I've become a contributor and I live in New York. First, there's an Open Forum, where anyone can write about whatever's on their mind. (Everyone has something on their mind, they just don't always get asked to express it. This is the chance you've been waiting for). Then there are Questions of the Issue that everyone is invited to answer. You can show a sense of humor or be as dry as a bone! The important thing is that you've contributed to the proceedings. Finally, a list of questions to consider for the next issue. See, it's fun. And before you even realize it, you've become a member of the club. Mmmmm... membership is good (drools like Homer Simpson).

**PONDER POND #8: A SOUP OF INTENSE THOUGHT**
D.B. Pedlar and A.S. Cruz
25727 Cherry Hill Rd.,
Cambridge Springs PA 16403
Price: free! (just ask) / Trades: yes
Size: 5.5 x 8.5" / Pages: 20

Like a couple of the other zines in this batch, here's one that actively encourages your creativity. (That might actually be a fairly radical notion, but I have a sneaking suspicion that everyone can handle it with only a minimal effort). The title is no mere affectation; you're invited to put your handheld device down and think for a bit. Then transfer your thinking to paper – I promise, it works; people have been doing that for centuries! – and submit it for publication. Each issue presents questions that everyone is invited to ponder. For example, here in #8, the pondering – as opposed to ponderous – festivities kick off with "What's the Deal with Disclaimers?" I cannot tell a lie, even though my name isn't George Washington: I was the one who submitted that entry. And from the Quirks of the English Language Department, musings on why "lord" isn't pronounced like "word". I'll tell you a secret: once you start thinking and, for that matter, pondering, you'll find it difficult to stop. But that would be a pandemic everybody could really benefit from.

Well, I really wanted to close this writing with a clever observation about Presidential Election 2020. But the deadline was November 1, so it had to be in two days before Election Day. I hope things went the way I wanted them to. If not, I see four more outrageously coiffed years ahead. Oops... did I just give my political preferences away? Well, as we say here in New York, waddaya gonna do? Or sometimes, when we feel like a little variety, we say, go fight City Hall. Meanwhile, tweeting Presidents and viral outbreaks (with or without a shortage of toilet paper aside), keep readin' zines. And do the right thing: send in letters of comment, for Pete's sake. You don't even have to know Pete personally.

**150 Pleasant St., #306**
**Easthampton, MA 01027**
**www.lcrw.net**
**info@lcrw.net**

Gavin J. Grant lives in Northampton, Massachusetts, with his family. He runs Small Beer Press and co-edits the zine **LADY CHURCHILL'S ROSEBUD WRISTLET** with his wife, Kelly Link. They also run a bookshop, Book Moon. Right now he should probably be making tomorrow's school lunch or walking the dog, or reading submissions for the press. He really appreciates everyone who wears masks when outside, thanks.

**THE GRASSHOPPERS ARE COMING!**
Alicia H., Bunny Ears Production
1600 Coal Ave., SE, Albuquerque, NM 87106
iknowbilly@gmail.com
iknowbilly.etsy.com ; patreon.com/iknowbilly
Price: $1 / Trades: likely
Size: 4.25" x 5.5" / Pages: 24

Loved this. Took me out of the present and current plague concerns and dropped me into… other plague concerns. It's short, but it turns from the locust plague into colonial ecological changes on this continent, using a lot of excerpts and black-and-white art along the way. It's a beautiful little zine. You should stuff an envelope with well concealed cash and send it off and get a copy of this. Good luck!

**I DON'T BELIEVE IN POPULAR KIDS: LESSONS FROM ONE GIRL'S FIGHT FOR INCLUSION**
Heather & Liz Gold
Microcosm Publishing
microcosmpublishing.com
Price: US $6.95; Can: $9.95 / Trades: ?
Size: 4.25" x 5.5" / Pages: 65

Should the world not have you in tears already, here's a zine to get you to tear up. Heather (a pseudonym, of course) is smart, 11-years-old, and somewhat different. She was bullied year after year from kindergarten on. The parents of the kids bullying her weren't particularly interested in the crappy behavior of their kids, so eventually Heather's mother, Liz, moved the kid to a new school. This is a story so common even if you don't have kids it will be familiar, but Heather's tenacity is something to behold.

**WATCH THE CLOSING DOORS #92**
Fred Argoff
Penthouse L, 1170 Ocean Pkwy
Brooklyn, NY 11230
Price: US$2.50 / Trades: ?
Size: 5.5" x 8.5" / Pages: 20

OK, you think you know what this is, but you are wrong. This issue is all about public transit but this time, it isn't about trains, it's buses. Pictures from all around the world, a bus from hell story — who doesn't have one? — and one thing that I found inspired: pictures of bus stops with hammocks in them. That is civilization.

**FROM SICK TO ILL: MIND OF A MANIC**
Donavan "Big 10" Gardner
big_10_gardner@yahoo.com
Microcosm Publishing
microcosmpublishing.com
Price: US$5.95; Can.: $7.99 / Trades:?
Size: 5.5" x 8.5" / Pages: 35

Donavan writes from a place he has worked hard to reach, position of strength from where he can write about where he has been and what it was like. A couple of years ago he was struggling with finding ways to live with his bipolar disorder and, as he writes here, he now has found a balance of medications and support that work for him.

**HEXCREEP//SEXFREAK**
August 2020
Salem Black
3A 762 St. Andre Drive
Orleans, ON K1C 456, Canada
Price: US$5; Can./Mex.: $5; World: $5 / Trades:? / Size: 5.5" x 8.5" / Pages: 16
Should you need a shot of gothic poetry, fear not, it is here.

**semibold.wordpress.com**
**im.semibold@gmail.com**
**twitter/instagram: @semibold**

**20X2 CHICAGO ZINE**
Andrew Huff & James Allenspach
Twitter & Instagram: @20x2chi
Price: $5 at Quimby's
Size: 8.5" x 11" / Pages: 24

In the Before Times, 20x2 was a monthly live performance series in Chicago, where 20 people would each have 2 minutes on stage to answer a question. After live performances bit the dust in the early spring, the two organizers decided to create a zine version. Twenty people were given one page each to answer the question, "What's your plan?" This was originally published in May, when we were only two months into this mess, and while there is a whole lot of uncertainty, there's still a sense of "temporary inconvenience" in most of the responses. I imagine if another issue were published right now, there might be a darker tone. Or maybe I'm projecting. Some of my favorite bits: a creative process flow chart, a plan written on a Post-it Note (where 1/3 of the Post-it Note is taken up by a drawing of a cat), a crossword puzzle, and a family trying to figure out how to play charades over Zoom.

**A PRESSING CONCERN BOOKMARK #2 EXCERPTS FROM THE RED RECORD: TABULATED STATISTICS AND ALLEGED CAUSES OF LYNCHING IN THE UNITED STATES, 1895, BY IDA B. WELLS-BARNETT**
Anne Elizabeth Moore
https://pressingconcern.onlineweb.shop/
Price: $6 each, a 6-issue subscription is $35
Size: 3" x 9" / Pages: 16

This tiny, bookmark-sized zine is no lightweight (which shouldn't be a surprise, based on the title). Ida B. Wells-Barnett is a Chicago legend. Born into slavery, she later became a teacher and an investigative journalist, focused on the hideous crime of lynching. Excerpted here are a few incidents from Wells-Barnett's pamphlet "The Red Record", where white women were shown to be complicit in the lynching of black men in order to save themselves from punishment or being ostracized in their own communities. In some ways, we have made very little progress in this country.

**UNDEREXPOSED: INNOVATORS OF CINEMA**
**VOL.1: CHANTAL AKERMAN**
**VOL. 3: PEDRO ALMODÓVAR**
Maddie Weiner
http://madelineweiner.com/
Akerman: Price: $2
Size: 5.5" x 8.5" / Pages: 12 pages
Almodóvar: Price $4
Size: 5.5" x 8.5" / Pages: 20

These are short, biographical comics about two great filmmakers. Maddie combines drawings with occasional photos and images, detailing their influences and the recurring themes and ideas in their films. While their film styles are quite different, both Akerman and Almodóvar primarily focus on stories about women's lives, and even though these aren't intended to be read together, I did find them to be interesting companion pieces. Maddie also provides extensive bibliography and filmography in each issue for further exploration.

**ELECTRON LIBRE #1**
Izalixe Straightheart
izalixe@gmail.com
Etsy.com/shop/izart
Patreon.com/izalixe
Price: $4 Canada / $5 US / $6 World
Size: 5.5" x 8.5" / Pages: 28

Formerly known as **THE HAPPY LONER**, Iza has changed the title of her zine to **ELECTRON LIBRE** ("Free Electron" in English), which she feels is a more accurate description of her mindset lately. In this issue, she shares her own experience of the COVID-19 lockdown in Canada. She was due for her annual trip to Vancouver right as things shut down. So she remained in Quebec and, like a lot of people, ended up doing a lot of cooking at home, going for long walks, doing more exercise at home, listening to a lot of podcasts, and thinking about the world around her. It's a well-rounded diary of a moment in time.

**LIBRARY EXCAVATIONS #9: CHICAGO'S FILED ARTISTS**

Marc Fisher
P.O. Box 12588, Chicago, IL 60612
publishers@halfletterpress.com
halfletterpress.com
Price: $6 / Size: 5.5" x 8.5" / Pages: 36

At the main branch of the Chicago Public Library lives the Chicago Artist Files. It's an archive of photos, news clippings, letters, artists' books, CDs, and other ephemera relating to 11,500 artists that anyone can access (and anyone can donate materials to.) The only requirement to be included in the archive is that an artist has had to have a minimum of two exhibits in Chicago. Marc writes about the history of the archive and shares some of his favorite findings in this high-quality, four-color printed zine, though, as he himself admits, this is just the barest scratch on the surface of what could be found here.

**FOUR ANECDOTES ABOUT DAVID BOWIE FROM MY OWN LIFE**

Joseph Carlough
joseph@displacedsnail.com
Displacedsnail.com
Price: $3 / Size: 3.5" x 5.5" / Pages: 24

Joseph shares four short anecdotes about Bowie – a co-worker who knew him; his earliest memory of Bowie; a Bowie-inspired Halloween costume; and a story about Joseph's memories of his family's cabin in the Poconos, where his musical taste was influenced by the old records his parents kept there. It's one of those zines that I wish were longer.

**I'VE WORN ALL THE SHIRTS IN THE DRAWER: 64 DAYS OF T-SHIRTS DURING COVID-19**

**GOT A BOX FULL OF T-SHIRTS… THE SEQUEL TO I'VE WORN ALL THE SHIRTS IN THE DRAWER**

Aj Michel
PO Box 877, Landsdowne, PA 19050
syndprod@gmail.com
syndprod.etsy.com
**SHIRTS IN THE DRAWER** Price: $5
Size: 5.5" x 4.25" / Pages: 68
**BOX FULL OF SHIRTS** Price: $3
Size: 4.25" x 5.5" / Pages: 20

As someone who has WAY too many t-shirts and a hard time parting with any of them, these two zines spoke to me. The first one is particularly poignant, because Aj wrote this in real time throughout the beginning of the pandemic, when we had no idea what was going to happen. We see things slowly unfold over time, even when we're just reading about t-shirts, there's always something more happening, too. Aj and I have one t-shirt in common, a Fountains of Wayne *Utopia Parkway* tour t-shirt. We were both devastated by the loss of Adam Schlesinger to this stupid fucking virus. If you're like me and you have a t-shirt problem, you will enjoy these zines.

**2140 Erma Drive**
**East Meadow, NY 11554**
**Passscribe@aol.com**
**kenbausertsnostalgicmuseum.blogspot.com/**
**thekenbausertchronicles.blogspot.com/**

**THE EAST VILLAGE INKY #62**
Ayun Halliday
Ayun@ayunhalliday.com
ayunhalliday.com
Price: $3. US / Trades: Inquire
Size: 4.25" x 5.5" / Pages: 40

It's fascinating to see how different people react to the COVID-19 pandemic through their zines; most seem content to just tell you what they've been doing during quarantine, while others – like Ayun – reminisce about what life was like before this "new normal." We learn how much she looks forward to being able to see movies at the Museum of Modern Art again, or eat at a favorite restaurant, or travel to some faraway place once more. She also gives thanks for all the proverbially small (but important) favors she's been blessed with, and admits to all the things she didn't accomplish during the many months of quarantine – like cleaning out a closet or learning another language. Yep! Lots of other cool stuff to read, of course.

If you're not acquainted with Ayun's zine, it's a hand-drawn and lettered mini that chronicles her life in NY fckn City, a place she loves dearly. It's a perennial favorite with readers so, if you've never seen it, you should really check it out.

**I'VE WORN ALL THE SHIRTS IN THE DRAWER**
Aj Michel
PO Box 877, Lansdowne, PA 13050
syndprod.etsy.com
Price: $5 (postpaid to USA) / Trades: (inquire) / Size: 4.5" x 5.5" / Pages: 36

Aj was relegated to working from home during the early months of the coronavirus outbreak, so she formulated a project. Because she has so many t-shirts, she decided to wear a different shirt every day until the drawer was empty or she went back to work at her office. Of course, she would photograph and tell a little story about each one. She also included a little blurb about what was happening in the world on each day's entry.

The shirts represent various interests and activities in Aj's life – everything from the Pines restaurant, where she'd have lunch with her parents back in the day, to a Dolly Dots band concert at the Milkboy venue to a Techniques audiophile branded tee.

Well, 64 days and 58 shirts later, she was still working from home, but the project had culminated in a great little zine called – what else? – **I'VE WORN ALL THE SHIRTS IN THE DRAWER**. Now, you can enjoy reading it as much as I did by sending Aj $5.

**GOT A BOX FULL OF T-SHIRTS**
Aj Michel
PO Box 877, Lansdowne PA 13050
syndprod.etsy.com
Price: $3 (postpaid to USA) / Trades: (inquire) / Size: 4.5" x 5.5" / Pages: 16

Unfortunately, the COVID-19 pandemic has lasted far longer than anyone would have wanted, so work-from-home orders have confined Aj Michel to a longer sentence. Luckily for us, it's also prompted her to produce a sequel to her earlier zine (**I'VE WORN ALL THE SHIRTS IN THE DRAWER**) and offer up **GOT A BOX FULL OF T-SHIRTS**, for your continued pleasure. Similar in scope but a little smaller in size than its predecessor, this newest endeavor examines a box full of old shirts that Aj was thinking of making into a quilt. Instead, she gives us a little history and the intended future of numerous subjects in the box. It's also available from the above address for only $3.

**HAPPY TAPIR #6**
Johnny Masiulewicz
happytapir1@gmail.com
https://www.etsy.com/listing/839646204/happy-tapir-6
Price: $4 US / Size: 5.5" x 8.5" / Pages: 48

Johnny Masiulewicz has released **HAPPY TAPIR #6**, subtitled "On the Make at the Drake", and it's all about the time he worked as a bellhop at the 100 year-old Chicago hotel. I always look forward to Johnny's zines, and this one exemplifies why. There are loads of interesting stories and personal experiences for your reading pleasure.

Quite a few celebrities stayed at the Drake back in the day, and Johnny got to meet many of them. One would stiff him on a tip, another was just arrogant, and still another left a very special suitcase for the staff to enjoy. Then there was his liaison with one of the higher-ups, and his eventual departure under less-than-ideal circumstances.

My wife happened to pick up this zine one day; after reading it for a while, she said, "There are some great stories in this one, but do you think they're all real?" I answered, "As far as I know, they're all real." I happened to send a message to Johnny, relaying Ro's question. He replied, "There is no fiction in the realm of **HAPPY TAPIR**."

**ELECTRON LIBRE #1**
Izalixe Straightheart
www.etsy.com/shop/izart
Price: $4 (Canada); $5 (USA) $6 (World) / Trades: inquire / Size: 8.5" x 11" / Pages: 24

Izalixe Straightheart used to produce a perzine called **THE HAPPY LONER**. For her latest effort, she's changed the name to **ELECTRON LIBRE** (French for "Free Electron") and released issue #1 in May 2020. Very similar to her earlier work, it features short stories about her life, including a couple of pages that she created some 15 years ago. Also mentioned in this issue is the Coronavirus (of course), and she tells us how it's affected her outlook on life. There are also some timely commentaries about podcasts and other zines, some photos and clip art scattered about, and two pages in French (in case you're bilingual).

**THE COURAGE PARTY**
www.microcosmpublishing.com
Price: $27 (hardcover/USA) / Trades: no
Size: 8" x 10" / Pages: 222

In preparation for this issue of **XEROGRAPHY DEBT**, Davida sent out a request for someone to review a new book, one she felt would be difficult for anyone to read or review due to its sensitive subject matter. I answered her request and received a copy of **THE COURAGE PARTY** in hardcover shortly thereafter.

Subtitled, "Helping Our Resilient Children Understand and Survive Sexual Assault", it's written by Joyce Brabner and illustrated by Gerta Oparaku. Some readers might remember Joyce from her marriage to

Harvey Pekar, originator of the *American Splendor* comic book series; she is also an actress and graphic novelist in her own right. It's co-written by Danielle, the subject of this latest work. It tells the story of a young girl who is sexually assaulted by an older boy and how she was able to deal with the trauma and eventually bring her attacker to justice.

Now, I'm perfectly aware of the fact that kids are growing up much faster than ever before. And, because of that, it's probably a lot easier to talk to them about sexuality and related subjects. But everyone is different, so I'm not sure that every kid would react to this story the same way, or be able to deal with it if it happened to them. And, at what age would it be appropriate to broach the topic? One age for one child, another age for a different kid, I'm thinking.

It's recommended that a parent and child read this book together; I think that would be best in most cases. But I also know that some adults would feel uncomfortable reading this book with a child. I'm also sure that some parents might not be able to deal with the reality of their child being sexually assaulted; they might even feel that it was somehow their kid's fault. Others might try to sweep it under the rug, feeling that the whole ordeal should just be forgotten; that to bring it out in the open would be an embarrassment to their family. In those cases, the child might bear a permanent emotional scar for the rest of their life.

So, I think it's a fine book; it's well written, and deals with a difficult subject and story in an admirable way. Whether it's the right book for your child to read – or for you to read with your child – is a matter you would have to decide. But I believe it's a great resource to have at your disposal if you want to prepare your kid for some of the unpleasantries of the real world – or if you find yourself in the same position as the subjects of this particular story.

**PURRSONAL MUSINGS #75**

R-Laurraine Tutihasi
PO Box 5323, Oracle, AZ 85623-5323
www.weasner.com
Price: $5 / Trades: Yes / Size: 8.5" x 11"
Pages: 16

The latest issue has some accounts of the drought conditions in Laurraine's part of the country and nearby wildfires. There are some photos of wildlife in and around her home as well as a couple of astronomical photos taken by her husband, Mike. A virtual trip to ReCONvene (topics included gaming, Climate Recovery, The Distant Future in Science Fiction, and Artificial Intelligence, among others) is reviewed, as well as some books and films seen lately. There is a readers column to close out his issue, mostly comments from (and in reply to) other members of the Stipple APA Laurraine belongs to.

**ALTERNATIVE INCITE #1**

Joe3
PO Box 3067, Laurel, MD 20709
joe3ofcp@gmail.com
Price: $3 / Trades: Inquire
Size: 7" x 8.5" / Pages: 40

According to its boilerplate, this zine "exists to encourage readers to follow their creative impulses and exercise their right to be bizarre, different, and/or peculiar in the interest of personal satisfaction and the greater good." That said, it's fairly conventional in its appearance but expertly assembled, with high quality printing standards and reproduction of photos. Its uniqueness comes mainly from the content and subject matter of the articles within; I found the writing and presentation to be excellent.

In the introduction, Joe3 points out the fact that Neo, a character in *The Matrix* movie, utters the expression, "Jesus Christ," in a particular scene, but the censors at American Movie Classics channel have overdubbed his voice to say, "Jeepers Creepers" when they aired it. Examining the idea that viewers might be offended by Neo's "use of the Lord's name in vain" makes for interesting reading.

Among the many other articles, you'll find things like, "Looking for a Way Off the Hamster Wheel," by J. Mathew Smith, essays on "The New Normal," "Walking Under a Stay-at-Home Order," and an interview with musician Suvo Sur, all by Joe3. I've only begun to scratch the surface here so I'd advise you cough up the three bucks required to order your own copy so you can explore this one further; I don't think you'll regret it.

**THE DESERT SUN #14**
Billy Roberts
1600 Coal Ave. SE, Albuquerque, NM 87106
Iknowbilly@gmail.com
Price: Donation / Trades: Inquire
Size: 8.5" x 11" / Pages: 2

Long associated with his other zines like, **LAST NIGHT AT THE CASINO** and **PROOF I EXIST**, Billy also produces a monthly newsletter-type offering called **THE DESERT SUN**; he asks for a yearly donation so figure something like $10 or $12 for 12 issues. In it, he keeps readers abreast of his (and wife Alicia's) latest activities; most recently that included moving from Baltimore back to Albuquerque, and then to a new address. This time around he also covers issues like water conservation, local New Mexican customs like Zozobra, the passing of Ruth Bader Ginsburg, his return to work at the casino, and the possibility of a Covid-19 vaccine, among other things. Yes, it's only two sides of a letter-sized piece of paper but Billy manages to fill it with a lot of worthwhile stuff.

**PONDER POND #8**
DB Pedlar
25727 Cherry Hill Rd.,
Cambridge Springs, PA 16403
Price: Free for the asking / Trades: Yes
Size: 5.5" x 8.5" / Pages: 20

Subtitled, "A Soup of Intense Thought," this issue continues the theme of asking readers to share their thoughts on topics raised in previous issues – or offer up new ideas in their submissions. There's a regular cast of creators like DB himself, A.S. Cruz, and Markell West, with several other contributors chiming in on questions like, "Is pride a good quality to have or is pride a signal that you are about to fall?" or "Should anti-abortionists offer to take care of unborn children once they are born?"

There are also some zine, movie and book reviews in this current issue. If you think this sounds like something you'd be interested in, why not send your zine in trade or order a copy? You can't beat the price.

**CHRISTIAN* NEW AGE QUARTERLY ISSUE: VOL. 24, NO. 4 (Autumn, 2020)**
Catherine Groves
PO Box 276, Clifton, NJ 07015-0276
info@christiannewage.com
Price: $3 (US) / Trades: inquire
Size: 7" x 8.5" / Pages: 36

**C*NAQ** is designed as a platform for different views on Christianity in order to promote the sharing of ideas and opinions on the subject. It's not designed to preach or chastise you for not going to church, but rather contains some worthwhile articles that can cause you to rethink some of your own beliefs.

This time around, Jacquie J. Higinbotham writes a great piece about "The Christ of the New Age," in which she laments the apparent loss in popularity of certain mainstream Protestant religions and their shrinking relevance in today's societies. "More and more people are identifying as spiritual but not religious," she says. Robert M. Price pens "Ritual in Space," a look at some episodes of Star Trek: The Next Generation and how some episodes seem to reference certain themes in the bible; and Joanne Winetzki writes about achieving harmony among diverse peoples through "Accepting Acceptance,." There are also some letters to the editor, classified ads, and a book review.

**ONCE BITTEN TWICE SHY THRICE A NIHILIST**

David Boone
worldofsimulacra@gmail.com
Price: Free / Trades: inquire
Size: 5.5 x 8.5 / Pages: 28

If you enjoy abstract poetry and prose you'll probably enjoy this zine; lots of cut & pasted photos, drawings, random quotes scattered about. Rather than try to decipher it all, I'll offer you a blurb from page 5: "Death is simply an absurd-seeming contingency on this absurd root fact of existence itself; why should anything even exist at all, much less us, and this?! And life can be seen as equally absurd – we have merely become more accustomed to it."

**OUT FROM THE VOID #3**

Brenton Gicker
outfromthevoid@yahoo.com
Price: Inquire / Trades: Inquire
Size: 5.5" x 8.5" / Pages: 32

Brenton is a registered nurse and emergency medical technician from Eugene, Oregon, and has put together a series of zines relating to the homeless, the mentally ill, and the dismal condition of our health care system in the US; this is issue **#3** of **OUT FROM THE VOID**.

There are numerous examples in this zine of people who need help but have largely nowhere to get it. I remember, back in the 1980s, President Reagan embarked on a campaign to deregulate the health care industry and, before you knew it, hospitals were closing up all over because they couldn't afford to stay in business. Several hospitals near me on Long Island, New York, closed – along with two huge psychiatric facilities, virtually throwing mentally ill patients out onto the street to fend for themselves. And people wonder why there are so many homeless? Well, this zine exposes the sorry conditions that have manifested themselves in the past 40 years.

There is a chapter here on how little help there is available for addiction sufferers; another story tells of Summer, a homeless and mentally ill woman who has a baby that is – fortunately – adopted by loving parents. There are also numerous resources listed in case you (or someone you know) need help from an agency to deal with mental health or addiction problems. This is a well-researched and first-hand collection of information that everyone should know, if for no other reason than to empower you to try and change the system. There is no price listed for the print version of this zine but you can email Brenton to inquire. I was able to find a complete copy through some online site and I doubt anyone would object to you simply going there to read it (simply Google the title with the number 3).

**I'M NOT FROM HERE I JUST LIVE HERE JULY & AUGUST, 2020**

Don Leach
1546 S.79th E. Ave., Tulsa, OK 74112
www.notmovingpictures.blogspot.com
notmovingpictures@gmail.com
Price: $1 each (US) / Trades: Inquire
Size: 8.5" x 11" / Pages: 2

I receive an issue of **I'M NOT FROM HERE I JUST LIVE HERE**, I think of how many times I've worn a shirt or a baseball cap from some city I've visited while on vacation, and someone will stop me in a store and say, "Oh, you must be a Red Sox fan" (because I'm wearing a tee-shirt from Boston). Truth is, I seldom wear a New York City-themed shirt even though I was born & raised there. Anyway, Don puts out this little two-pager every month or two and fills it with whatever's on his mind at the time. He doesn't list a price on it but I imagine a dollar would get you a copy; he'd probably make a trade for your zine as well. I currently have two issues so I figured I'd lump them together.

In July he was especially concerned with the Covid-19 virus (weren't we all?) and President Trump. He was in the middle of working on several other zines (I'm looking forward to seeing those), reading a whole bunch of zines and manga from other people, and watching lots of Netflix. There's also his take on trading zines with other people and the possibility of visiting Japan once this pandemic is over.

For August Don writes about some trips his family has taken and the need to continue to wear makes while traveling. Recent destinations have included Natural Falls State Park; Galena & Coffeeville, Kansas; and the Totem Park in Chelsea, Oklahoma. There are more updates on the other zines he's been working on as well as some brief reviews of music and movies.

In his most recent mailing, Don included a mini-zine with some haiku. I must admit, I'm not the biggest poetry fan but I really thought he had some good stuff in this collection. If you're ordering something from him, include another dollar and ask for it as well.

**WORTH A WASHINGTON! ISSUE: #27 (AUGUST 2020)**

Markell Raphaelson West
address: 115 Irving Street,
Laurel, MD 20707-4503
markellorhighwater@gmail.com
Price: $1 (US) / Trades: Yes
Size: 8.5" x 11" / Pages: 11

With over a dozen contributors, this is starting to resemble an APA (Amateur Press Association). I've seen several issues thus far and the format seems to have stabilized; there are questions or subjects you are asked to answer or give your opinion on. You may also post questions of your own that you'd like others to respond to; the following issue will contain responses from whomever felt compelled to reply. There's now an open forum where you're invited to write anything you'd like; I imagine others will offer feedback on whatever you've written.

A typical question found in this issue: "What do you think of the Washington Redskins changing their name?" Condensed replies ranged from, "I think it's way overdue," to "I think it's an exhausted subject," to "I'm uncomfortable that they're being pressured into it." While the actual replies are much more in-depth and contemplative, I think you get the idea.

If exchanging ideas with other people on a wide variety of subject matter interests you, please check this one out. It's free online and available in print form for a dollar (or anything with a Washington on it) or a written correspondence.

**THIS ZINE HAS ISSUES #2**

Dave Combs
Microcosm Publishing,
2752 N. Williams Ave., Portland, OR 97227
www.Microcosm.Pub
Price: $4 (US), $6 (Canada) / Trades: No
Size: 5.5" x 8.5" / Pages: 40

Subtitled, "Breaking The Stigma of Mental Illnesses," this particular issue deals with anxiety. It's professionally laid out and impressive in appearance; there are numerous stories, poetry, photos, original artwork, and illustrations from over a dozen and a half contributors.

Among the many topics addressed are "Inside a Panic Attack; What it's like When Anxiety Strikes," "Anxiety Therapy," and "Anxiety and Covid-19." In "Effects of Anxiety," Allison Leonard tells of how her job as an insurance claims adjuster caused her to feel the effects of anxiety after dealing with customers who'd had accidents. She began to see how easy it was for someone else to cross over that double yellow line in the center of the highway and collide head-on with her. Her anxiety then caused her to begin driving slowly and so timidly that she herself might create problems on the road.

There are many other offerings here that make for great reading. If you, or someone you know, suffers from anxiety, this might be a good introduction to the subject.

**MARK TIME #134**

Mark Strickert
PO Box 1171, Rialto, CA. 92377
busnrail@yahoo.com
Price: $2 (US) / Trades: Yes
Size: 8.5" x 11" / Pages: 8

Mark's latest offering is a different kind of auto-biography; subtitled, "Travel in the Time Before MarkTime," it uses short stories relating to his travels from the mid '60s to 1990 to chronicle his life during that timeframe. For example, the first trip he has any memory of was to the Wisconsin Dells with his parents and siblings; of course, he adds a little description of the area or brief reminiscences about what happened in each place.

I found it to be quite interesting, overall, and it also reminded me that Mark "collects" things like states and counties (he keeps a record of all the places he's visited) so it was probably easier for him to write this essay than most other folks. Who else would remember that their first California visit was in October, 1978, or that they flew up to Toronto with their sister in late 1979? This issue also has some photos relating to his previous issue (#133). A fun read, for sure; check it out!

**ANACHRONISMS #6**

Fred Argoff
1170 Ocean Parkway (Penthouse L),
Brooklyn, NY 11230-4060
Price: $2 (US) / Trades: Inquire
Size: 5.5" x 8.5" / Pages: 20

We've all got a right to complain about that which we feel is unfair, poorly designed or made, and annoying. The latest issue of **ANACHRONISMS** is Fred's outlet for blowing off steam or pointing out the senseless things in life. This time around, he's got a dozen items that have been bugging him. Maybe you share his feelings about the excessive use of euphemisms, cars that have grown too smart for their own good, and notices that warn you that the warranty on your car is expiring – even when you don't own a car!

One of Fred's rants in this issue hit a little closer to home for me. He originally got to love using Adobe PageMaker, a word-processing and page layout app, when he worked for a particular company in the past. Well, it turns out that I, too, was a PageMaker fan; I found it to be easy to navigate and filled with great features. But, years later, when Fred tried to use PageMaker with his Windows 10 operating system he discovered that they were incompatible. Before he went too ballistic trying to get it to work, he was fortunate to discover and learn to use Microsoft Office – almost as good as PageMaker – so his story had a happy ending. In my case, Adobe stopped making PageMaker for the newer Mac operating systems and I had to buy their Creative Suite with InDesign – their replacement for PageMaker. Ironically, I still feel PageMaker was much easier to use and had better features than InDesign so it's my turn to bitch about something here.

**PRISON SENTENCES; WORDS FROM WITHIN GUARDED SPACES**
Roxanne Aubrey Marina
140 10th Street South, La Crosse, WI 54601
rox@ope.pub
Price: $7 (US) / Trades: Inquire
Size: 4" x 6" / Pages: 24

This is a neat little booklet, hand-assembled with thread binding it at the spine, containing beautiful illustrations by Tiana Traffas. It features the work of Ken Amen, a poet prisoner originally from Kisli, Kenya, and a prison reform activist, Elizabeth Hawes – both members of the 1,200-person strong Minnesota Prison Writing Workshop. Ken has previously won a Broadside Award and been nominated for a Pushcart prize for his writing. Elizabeth is an award-winning writer, gardener, and dancer.

I found Ken's poetry to be very thoughtful and intense, yet easy to understand; most relating to his early life spent in and around African villages. I felt transposed to another continent reading his words. I was especially enamored with Elizabeth's stories. Her writing conveys the aura of someone to whom the craft comes easily; her ideas, style, and structure impress me as an art form. I would love to read more of her work. Overall, this is a small but really fine collection.

## kris mininger

**Calvo Sotelo 13B, 4B, Plasencia 10600, Cáceres, Spain**
**kmininger@gmail.com**

Hola amigos. Half of the zines I reviewed this time around should've been reviewed for the last issue, but, well, maybe you've heard... Shit's kind of crazy at the moment. Better late than never. Also, I have a new zine available. It's called **TOOLS ON TOUR**. It's about a little road trip I took last November (when travel was still a thing) helping a friend transport his combination machine from Ireland to Finland. If we've traded in the past keep an eye on your mailbox. If not, five bucks should do the trick. Now if you'll excuse me, I have a kitten in desperate need of cuddles.

**WE'LL NEVER HAVE PARIS #16: FOOD**

Andria Alefhi, editor
Available from Antiquated Future
PO Box 42081 Portland, OR 97242
neverhaveparis@gmail.com
antiquatedfuture.com
www.wellneverhaveparisszine.com
Price: $6 US / Trades: No
Size: 4.25" x 5.5" / Pages: 44

"**WNHP** is an annual journal of nonfiction memoir in zine format." This is a nifty little publication with crisp, clean layout and design. (And nice paper to boot.) In this issue, all about food, nine contributors wax poetic about subjects as diverse as the Filet-O-Fish sandwich, the dreaded endive, hunting and gathering at the local farmers market, hearing the news at the breakfast table that Freddy Mercury passed away, and much more. I really enjoyed this zine. In fact, I enjoyed it so much I picked up a few back issues (**#13: WEST COAST, #14: AWAY, #15: AMERICA**). Next issue's theme is Hindsight. Looking forward to it.

**I'VE WORN ALL THE SHIRTS IN THE DRAWER: 64 DAYS OF T-SHIRTS DURING COVID-19**

A.j. Michel
PO Box 877, Lansdowne PA 19050
syndprod@gmail.com
syndprod.etsy.com
Price: $5 US / Trades: Inquire
Size: 5.5" x 4.25" / Pages: 68

During the early days of the pandemic A.j. had an idea while doing the laundry. She had received word from her job that she was to work from home until further notice. So, "what if I wore a different shirt every day (…), took pictures, wrote about them, and made a zine? (…) It was a project with a fixed beginning and end, something I could control during this downward spiral." If you're familiar with A.j.'s other zines then you already know that the end result is a work of art. She tells the story behind 58 t-shirts and includes an image of each one. The text is a mix of nostalgia and anxiety. The shirts bring back memories of bands seen, cons attended, and radio stations listened to over the years. Her consumption of the daily news triggers fear, anger, and frustration. This is an important little document. And the Philadelphia Record Exchange t-shirt made me homesick for my university days in Philly. God, I miss record stores. And cheesesteaks.

**GOT A BOX FULL OF T-SHIRTS: THE SEQUEL TO I'VE WORN ALL THE SHIRTS IN THE DRAWER**

A.j. Michel
PO Box 877, Lansdowne PA 19050
syndprod@gmail.com
syndprod.etsy.com
Price: $3 US / Trades: Inquire
Size: 4.25" x 5.5" / Pages: 16

But wait, there's more! After A.j. finished the **I'VE WORN ALL THE SHIRTS IN THE DRAWER** project she lugged a box full of t-shirts out of storage that she was vaguely hoping to turn into a quilt or a blanket one day. This time around she didn't wear the shirts, but randomly pulled them out and wrote about them. This is another nifty little zine with fantastic layout and design that you should get your hands on before they're all gone. Added bonus: I learned about the existence of the movie *Tapeheads*. Reading zines makes you smarter.

**KNOW-IT-ALL ASSHOLE JERK**

Adel Souto
adel.156.souto@gmail.com
adelsouto.com

Price: $5 US / Trades: No
Size: 8.5" x 5.5" / Pages: 56

Pranksters, performance artists, wild-eyed prophets, and half-assed hoaxsters abound in this one. **KNOW-IT-ALL ASSHOLE JERK** reminds me a bit of the Australian zine **BIZARRISM**, but instead of deep dives into the weird and obscure, Adel gives the reader short, tantalizing snippets that send you running to the computer to look for more information about all this crazy shit. For example: the Circumcellions (a Berber Christian cult), the art of trepanation, tiny postage stamps from Bhutan that are playable 33 1/3 rpm records, the UMMO UFO hoax, and much more. And if your curiosity still isn't satisfied when you finish reading the zine check out Adel's blog. You won't be disappointed. (One of Adel's recent blog posts is about a conspiracy theory that Finland doesn't exist. Seriously, what the hell is going on out there?)

**READY FOR WAR: THE FLORIDA EDITION**
Adel Souto
adel.156.souto@gmail.com
adelsouto.com
Price: $5 US / Trades: No
Size: 8.5" x 5.5" / Pages: 54

When I ordered a copy of **KNOW-IT-ALL ASSHOLE JERK** I was pleasantly surprised to find that Adel slipped a copy of **READY FOR WAR: THE FLORIDA EDITION** in the envelope as well. This zine is fairly straightforward: 48 color photos of battle jackets or cut-offs (or kuttes as they are known in heavy metal subcultures) that Adel took on the streets of Miami and at concerts in Florida. I was surprised to see the "European features are NOT the pinnacle of BEAUTY" and ""FIGHT EVIL. READ BOOKS." patches mixed in with the Motörhead and Iron Maiden patches. The metalheads I knew in high school weren't that progressive. This is the kind of thing I wouldn't have sent off for after reading a review, but now that I'm holding it in my hands and I can see the high production values I'm giving it a solid two thumbs up. Check it out.

**BIBLIO-CURIOSA #9**
Chris Mikul
PO Box K546, Haymarket NSW 1240, Australia
chris.mikul88@gmail.com
Price: $10 World / $7 Australia / Trades: No
Size: 5.5" x 8.5" / Pages: 52

A meticulously researched zine completely devoted to unusual writers and strange books. This time around Chris focuses on autobiographies and memoirs. He takes the reader on a wild journey into the weird and wonderful lives of Irish magician Seamus Burke (*From the Earth to a Star)*, the "Wild Woman of Butte" Mary MacLane (*Men Who Have Made Love to Me*), the "Hermit of Peking" Sir Edmund Backhouse (*Décadence Mandchoue*), and much more. The article on the life and times of G. Gordon Liddy completely blew my mind. How is this guy not behind bars? And as always there are lots of full-color images of eccentric writers and their book covers. Great stuff.

**FOUR YEAR DEPRESSION: HOW TO LOVE YOUR FAMILY (EVEN THOUGH THEY VOTED FOR YOU-KNOW-WHO)**
Billy McCall
1600 Coal Ave. SE, Albuquerque, NM 87106
**(Note the new address)**
iknowbilly@gmail.com
Price: $10 US / Trades: No
Size: 5.5" x 8.5" / Pages: 96

Billy, publisher of the zines **LAST NIGHT AT THE CASINO** and **PROOF I EXIST**, has written a book. It's about the despair that set in when Trump came to power and the daily struggle to remain hopeful throughout it all. I was born and raised in the US, but I haven't lived there since George W. Bush was in his first term. That doesn't mean I can ignore or escape the nightmare of the last 3-1/2 years. And like everybody else, I'm suffering from Trump fatigue. I press the mute button every time he's on the news.

This book is also an unflinching look into addiction, the complicated relationship Billy has with his family, and how infuriating it is to watch people vote for politicians who are clearly not going to do anything to improve their lives. The fact that Billy had the energy and will power to sit down and write this book without becoming physically ill is nothing short of courageous. Highly recommended.

**NOT MY SMALL DIARY #20: THE POWER OF MUSIC**

Delaine Derry Green, editor
MySmallDiary.etsy.com
mysmallwebpage.com
Price: $6.50 / Trades: No
Size: 5.5" x 8.5" / Pages: 136

As the pandemic drags on I find it harder and harder to keep my attention fixed on what I'm reading so I've been spending more time listening to music. Putting on headphones and rediscovering albums I haven't listened to for ages is a pleasant way of escaping reality. (And it's easier to listen to music than hold a book in front of my face now that I have a kitten that loves nothing more than taking a nap on my chest every time I crash on the sofa at the end of the day.) So a zine about the power of music couldn't have come at a better time.

This time around Delaine gives us autobiographical comics from 54 artists and writers. There are tales of making mix tapes, meeting the Beatles, playing in bands, attending life-changing concerts, and so much more. Peter Conrad's tale of taping a song off of a college radio station and not being able to find out who the artist was for decades, until the internet came around, is hilarious. Carrie McNinch's comic about playing some of her father's favorite songs for him as he went through the final stages of Alzheimer's is absolutely heartbreaking. By the way, at $6.50 this is the bargain of the century. And it comes with a cool guitar pick!

**COMMUNICATING VESSELS #30 (SUMMER 2020)**

Anthony Walent
PO Box 2048, Tucson, AZ 85702
Price: Donation (US cash or stamps preferred) / Trades: Inquire
Size: 6.5" x 8.5" / Pages: 38

**COMMUNICATING VESSELS** is one of those rare journals of art, poetry, and anarchy beautifully printed on an old salvaged press that you don't see too often these days. (If you're familiar with **THE MATCH!** or **THE CUNNINGHAM AMENDMENT** you'll know what I'm talking about.) There's a lot of ground covered in this issue: Anthony's love/hate relationship with Tucson and how he ended up in Arizona; romantic tales of hidden treasure inspired by a recent hike in the Superstition Mountains; the importance of living in harmony with nature.

As always there are lots of letters and zine reviews, as well as references to the works of Brueghel, Bosch, Cervantes, and Rabelais. I always take my time with each issue of **CV**, savoring the words and images as I drift off into daydreams of wandering the countryside with a donkey and a wineskin as my companions. And the smell of the ink on the pages brings back memories of my year working for a printer in my late teens, loading giant sheets of paper into a massive five color Heidelberg, being half stoned from breathing in that solvent soaked air all day long… Ah, the good old days…

### I'M NOT FROM HERE I JUST LIVE HERE #FEB/APRIL 2020, #MAY/JUNE 2020, #JULY 2020, #AUGUST 2020

Don Leach
1546 S 79th E Ave., Tulsa, OK 74112
notmovingpictures@gmail.com
notmovingpictures.blogspot.com
Price: Donation / Trades: Yes
Size: 8.5" x 11" / Pages: 2

This is a short perzine about Don's life and adventures in Tulsa. Work woes, Covid-19 stress, Black Lives Matter, a brief road trip… And long lists of what Don's been reading, listening to, and watching. Also included with these issues were a couple of mini-zines: **AWESOME: A (VERY) SHORT STORY** about racism, and **DOES THIS COUNT? (POETRY FROM A NON-POET)** which contains the fantastic haiku, "Called me boring, Because I couldn't fake cheer, Married you anyway". I always enjoy opening an envelope and having lots of little zines and things slide out across the table. It's inspiring and always reminds me how incredibly unproductive I am with my zine output.

### THE KEN CHRONICLES #56

Ken Bausert
2140 Erma Drive, East Meadow, NY 11554
passcribe@aol.com
thekenbausertchronicles.blogspot.com
Price: $3 US hardcopy / $2 US PDF / $4 Can/Mex/World hardcopy
Trades: Letter of comment or contact suggested
Size: 5.5" x 8.5" / Pages: 28

How many zines make it to issue #56? Well done, sir. Ken is a retired mechanic who splits his time between NY and FL. This time around, in the regular column "People, Places and Things (that aren't there anymore)," Ken writes about a friend who recently passed away, a beloved food truck from the old days, and a beautiful house from the old neighborhood that got torn down by developers. We also get Ken's thoughts on Covid-19, making a will, Black Lives Matter, and some useful gardening tips. The color image of Ken's Neptune green Smith-Corona portable typewriter, which has been in his possession since he was in grade school, made me, well, Neptune green with envy. What a beauty!

There is lots of friendly back and forth in the lengthy letters section, and that's really what this zine feels like: a long letter from an old friend. Ken also gives us the rundown on what's he's been reading, listening to, and watching lately. And his article about comparing prices of different brands of memory foam online had me in stitches: "But, by now, you've likely figured out that I wouldn't be writing this article if it was that simple." Always a great read.

**P.O. Box 477553**
**Chicago, IL 60647-7553**
**caboosezine@gmail.com**

My friend Julie and I finished **CUL-DE-SAC #8**, and it's available at a few different places like my Etsy store (my shop is LizMasonZines). This issue is the Past Lives issue since all the pieces in it are about places that have closed or hobbies or people we've given up. I wrote a eulogy to the closing of my favorite deli, a review of a movie my friends and I used to watch at slumber parties (which is actually a piece about dance battles) and an admission that I broke up with someone because he didn't like *The Matrix* (somehow I had a lot to say about that [?!] ), and Julie wrote about going to *Supernatural* conferences (as in the TV show) and the withdrawal she experienced after Toys R Us closed. It seems extra poetic that the theme would be Past Lives in light of you know, pre/post COVID — the pieces were actually written before the pandemic even started. Anyway, I'm pretty proud of this issue.

**IS IT JUST ME OR ARE WE NAILING THIS? ESSAYS ON BOJACK HORSEMAN**
Molly E. Simas , M.L. Schepps , Joshua James Amberson, Various
antiquatedfuture@gmail.com
antiquatedfuture.com
Price: $5.00US
Size: 5.5"x8.5" / Pages: 68

I'm always a sucker for thoughtful and philosophical writing about popular culture, whether I'm familiar with the topic or not. Sure, I've seen some episodes of *Bojack Horseman* but by no means all of it. The writing in this zine is so good that it doesn't matter. Most of these pieces do what some of my favorite writing about popular culture does: they communicate truths that are relevant to the universal human experience, independent of medium.

**MAGICAL SPACES #1: AN INCOMPLETE HISTORY OF LONG-GONE ILLEGAL PUNK VENUES IN BOSTON FROM 2000 TO 2015**
Chris Strunk
antiquatedfuture.com
Price: $8 US / Size: 5.5"x8.5" / Pages: 40

This zine is part of Free the Future Press's "Magical Spaces" series. Chris spent 15 years going to shows or performing at shows in Boston ("or somewhere around there"). He was afraid the details would be lost to the sands of time. Hence the zine. Police, mold, fire hazards — all the things you expect from DIY spaces and the requisite adventures contained therein, and they do not disappoint. Of course it's the narrator's personal details that I find the most amusing, such as the his admission that he drank too much chocolate brandy at the Ashford Street House and smashed up the toilet.

**GOT A BOX FULL OF T-SHIRTS...**
A.j. Michel
syndprod@gmail.com
etsy.com/shop/syndprod
Price: $3 US / Size: 4"x5.5" / Pages: 16

Aka **THE SEQUEL TO I'VE WORN ALL THE SHIRTS IN THE DRAWER** (which is equally entertaining), A.j. uses some quarantine time to meditate on their t-shirt collection, a zine that's part perzine, part listicle, part cultural criticism, full delight. And of course it's a peek into A.j.'s pop culture interests and personal history. As with anything by this zine veteran, recommended.

**USED RECORDS AND TAPES #1**
Issue #/Date: #1
Chris Auman and Mike Dixon
(RoosterCow Press)
reglarwiglar.com
Price: $7 US / Size: 8.5"x5.5" / Pages: 40

Reports of the deaths of all sorts of things are greatly exaggerated: vinyl, tapes, CDs record stores, print. Chris and Mike write about some gems they picked up in any number of these formats: Asia, Flock of Seagulls, The Thompson Twins. Part music zine, part perzine, 100% fun.

**HOMICIDE: BUCKTOWN 9 MURDERS FROM 2002-2018 POLICE REPORTS AND PHOTOGRAPHS**
Samuel T. Logan
quimbys.com
Price: $15 US / Size: 11"x8.5" / Pages: 36

How nice! Someone did a zine about nine murders in my neighborhood and it wasn't me. It includes photos and police records of the scene post-crime, and I recognized all the places. Guess I know what places to avoid now, which is apparently pretty much everywhere in the immediate blocks around my house, which just goes to show that even if you feel comfortable you never know what happens when you're around. Well, if you don't hear from me in the next issue maybe I neglected to avoid the right intersection. Sam's other issue of **HOMICIDE** gives the same treatment to Wicker Park, the neighborhood next to me. Planning on visiting Chicago? Why not pick up these great Chicago souvenirs at Quimby's, conveniently located smack dab on the border between Bucktown and Wicker Park?



**ALTERNATIVE INCITE: ISSUE #1**
Joe Smith (aka Joe3)
P.O. Box 3067; Laurel, MD 20709
joe3ofcp@gmail.com or, to purchase,
Paypal to manualpubs@yahoo.com
www.butter-lamb.com
Price: $3.00 per issue / Trades: ?
Size: 8.5" x 5.5" / Pages: 40 (including covers)
Description: **ALTERNATIVE INCITE** (tag line/ slogan: "Follow the creative impulse") exists to encourage readers to follow their creative impulse and exercise their right to be bizarre, different, and/or peculiar in the interest of personal satisfaction and the greater good.

This first issue is mostly written by Joe, who is a funny writer who lets you into his world. With great personal insight, he discusses censorship, etymology, privacy, and a good variety of topics, often based on books and articles he's read. There also the first in a series of interviews with people who are following their creative impulses. Who knows? You might be next!

This is an engaging publication, with eye-pleasing fonts and intriguing photographs. It is insightful enough that I keep thinking of it as **ALTERNATIVE INSIGHT**, but I'm mistaken! **ALTERNATIVE INCITE** is well worth the requested $3.00!

**ANACHRONISMS III**
Fred Argoff
Penthouse L; 1170 Ocean Parkway;
Brooklyn, NY 11230-4060
Price: $2.00 / Trades: unspecified (but it wouldn't surprise me a bit)
Size: 8.5" x 5.5" / Pages: unnumbered but I am nice and I counted them: 20, including covers
Description: 11 delightful essays, with illustrations

I love this collection of Fred's descriptions of artifacts and how they're changing with the times. (I don't want to spoil the fun so I'll leave it at that!)

**BROOKLYN #110**
Fred Argoff
Penthouse L; 1170 Ocean Parkway;
Brooklyn, NY 11230-4060
Price: $10.00 for four quarterly issues (cash only!!!) / Trades: unspecified (but it wouldn't surprise me a bit) / Size: 8.5" x 5.5"
Pages: unnumbered but I am nice and I counted them: 24, including covers
Description: Brooklyn History

This is a special themed issue about Brooklyn history, which, Fred assures us, is an interesting subject. He talks about East New York as being Hollywood before there was a Hollywood.

Get this issue to learn a lot, including:

- What toy, candy, and meat product were invented in Brooklyn?
- Why is Liberty Avenue called Liberty Avenue?
- Why does Kings Highway meander across Brooklyn crazily?
- Who is this man?
- Why was Walt Whitman fired as editor of the *Brooklyn Eagle*?
- What is this thing?
- What is a terminal moraine?
- What is better than Pickle Day? Okay—I'll spill the beans on that last one. What's better than Pickle Day? Apparently, having a brand-new subscription to **BROOKLYN!**

**THE C♥URAGE PARTY: HELPING OUR RESILIENT CHILDREN UNDERSTAND AND SURVIVE SEXUAL ASSAULT**
Microcosm Publishing
2752 N Williams Ave., Portland, OR 97227
orders@microcosmpublishing.com
https://microcosmpublishing.com/catalog/books/10335
Price: 27.95 (Special price for people working with at-risk children: $15.00) / Trades: no / Size: 8" x 10" / Pages: 220
Description: Illustrated hardcover book for children to read with adults

I couldn't put this down. I love books that teach me something new—I'd never heard of a courage party! It is a very engaging book, telling a real story about sexual assault with details and humor. It has delightful illustrations.

By the way, I'm not sure why this isn't called **THE CO♥RAGE PARTY**, since the heart looks more like the U than the O. (Just as I've never understood why Valentines often use the word "I♥ve" instead of the word "lo♥e.")

Anyhow, there are a few other questionable formatting and punctuation choices, and, although the authors indicated that they wanted to teach the real words for body parts, they define penis as "boy genitals" and vagina as "girl genitals." That's a little too simplistic, especially after they make such a big deal of using the correct terminology and "dictionary words."

Otherwise, I wholeheartedly recommend this page-turner.

**DETOX YOUR PLACE**

Microcosm Publishing
2752 N Williams Ave., Portland, OR 97227
orders@microcosmpublishing.com
https://microcosmpublishing.com/catalog/books/10584
Price: $14.95 / Trades: no
Size: 4 5" x 7" / Pages: 192
Description: softcover book about how to live safely

I found this very hard to read, with about seven syntax errors on page one. This was kind of a blessing in disguise, since I ended up skimming the whole book, and it would have been too depressing to read it in detail. It's a book about how everything in my house will blind me (or at least poison me).

My husband is extremely gratified to see that he's not the only Prognosticator of Doom in the world. This book may ruin your life, as you'll have to change your ways and means—but then it will save your life.

**"AWESOME: A (VERY) SHORT STORY" (JULY 2020)**

Don Leach
1546 S. 79th E. Avenue; Tulsa, OK 74112
notmovingpictures@gmail.com
www.notmovingpictures.blogspot.com
Price: not for sale / Trades: trade or stamps or a dollar
Size: 4.25" x 5.5" / Pages: 4
Description: A (Very) Short Story: "This is a work of fiction, born from my desire to comment but the only way I feel I can do that is as an observer."

This is just a draft of the story, there's nothing fundamental to be changed. It rang true to me, and I didn't realize it was fiction until I read the comment at the end! An engaging, uplifting story about racism.

**DITHERING DOODLES #99**

Steve Anderson
259E 700S; Salt Lake City, UT 84111
premiumdeluxe@hotmail.com
Price: $2.00 / Trades: Yes (Steve adds "or free if unemployed)
Size: 8.5" x 5.5" / Page count: 20
Description: "From Salt Lake City to Dah Moon!"

This one begins with a clever intro, of the Dithering Dood emerging from a rock. If you have a tolerance for seeing cartoon characters in their underwear, this issue is for you! (At least they're tasteful boxers.)

This issue includes reminiscences of watching the moon landing with his grandparents, and, of course, the usual gleeful drawings and letterings (with the occasional tasteless drawing). It still makes me smile!

**THE LETTER EXCHANGE #53**

Gary and Lorna
lexinfo@letter-exchange.com
www.letter-exchange.com
Price: $23.00 for 3 issues
Size: 8.5" x 5.5" / Pages: 32 pages
Description: pen-pal listings and articles about letter-writing

As always, this issue has a wonderful variety of listings for people who are looking for correspondents and correspondence. The listings include specific requests, questions, and offers for penship.

There are articles about letter-writing and delivery, as well as letters to the editor and a question for you to answer in the next issue: How is the pandemic affecting your mail, and do you have ideas for what can be done about it? Send in letters to **LEXS** for the Winter 2021 issue on this and lots of other topics related to letters, postcards, and correspondence in general by December 15.

**PONDER POND #7**

D.B. Pedlar
25727 Cherry Hill Road;
Cambridge Springs, PA 16403
Price: Readers are free to add their pondering to the topics already pondered / Trades: Yes
Size: 8.5" x 5.5" / Pages: 20
Description: Letters of Comment, Zine Reviews, and Discussion Questions and Ponderings

Zine reviews, amusing verse by A.J. Cruz, and some points pondered/to ponder, including moon colonies and quirks of English.

Always an enjoyable read with nice illustrations.

**PONDER POND #8**

D.B. Pedlar
25727 Cherry Hill Road; Cambridge Springs, PA 16403
Price: Readers are free to add their pondering to the topics already pondered / Trades: Yes
Size: 8.5" x 5.5" / Pages: 20
Description: Letters of Comment, Book Reviews, and Discussion Questions and Ponderings

According to D.B., this one is not suitable for children. (Who am I to say?) Discussion of disclaimers, the English language, beer, abortion, and other issues.

Have I mentioned that I always enjoy this zine?

**THRIFTY TIMES #52**

Sarah B. MacDonald
Email address: thriftytimes@aol.com
www.thriftyzine.com or Etsy.com
Price: $13.00 for 12 issues
Size: 8.5" x 5.5" / Pages: 16
Description: adventures in thrift-store shopping

After a 3-month hiatus in thrifting because of the pandemic, Sarah and Nick are back to their old tricks, thrift-shopping and cartooning about it. This issue features 10 free and fun things to do other than thrifting, just in case your local thrift store isn't open yet.

As always, there's a "From the Kitschen" recipe, this time from the *Hunt's Complete Tomato Sauce Cookbook*. The Book Look this time is about *First in Thirst*, about the history of Gatorade. I haven't been thrift shopping in even longer than 3 months, but this may just send me to eBay to do some lazy shopping of my own. In any case, **THRIFTY TIMES** is a nice vicarious trip to the thrift store!

**LADY CHURCHILL'S ROSEBUD WRISTLET #40**

Small Beer Press
150 Pleasant Street, #306;
Easthampton, MA 01027
smallbeerperss@gmail.com
smallbeerpress.com/lcrw
Price: $20 / 4 issues / Trades: I can't imagine so.
Size: 8.5" x 5.5" / Pages: 60
Description: Their description: "A twice-yearly burst of fantastic fiction, poetry, and a cooking column."

I enjoyed this issue, especially Mary Cool's cool short story "The Fruit That Bears the Flower," but there is a great variety of fiction here. I even enjoyed the poetry (a set of related and titled haikus). Clever! The cooking column by Nicole Kimberling, "We Should See Less of Each Other," was a second-person chat with Sodium. You won't find a step-by-step recipe here, but you'll definitely have fun reading it and come away with ideas for a future cooking adventure.

There is an impressive set of 12 options for subscribers, ranging from 4 electronic issues for $9.95 to $2,500 for everything they publish from now on. This includes their "Chocolate City" subscription ($35.00), which includes a good chocolate bar each time. I can't vouch for the goodness of the chocolate, since either Davida didn't receive one or she ate it before sending me the zine. However, I've never had a bad chocolate bar that wasn't from the Soviet Union, so if you pay the $38 for the "Choc City" subscription, I think you're pretty safe.

**SHARDS OF GLASS IN YOUR EYE! #7 (AUGUST 2012)**

Kari Tervo
P.O.B. 7831, Beverly Hills, CA 90212
shardsofglassinyoureye@gmail.com
www.etsy.com/shop/SweetMayhemZinery
Price: $3.00 / Trades: ask first
Size: 8.5" x 5.5" / Pages: 28 pages
Description: Perzine/humor zine with puzzles

Kari is a psychologist and comedienne with a healthy dose of whimsy. This zine contains original puzzles, humorous diary entries, and unique columns such as "Seven Celebrities I Have Seen in Their Natural Environment."

This is written by Kari, including a spoof article by a celebrity. Kari has also printed some correspondence she's gotten. Most life-changing for me was an item in "Miss Kari's Etiquette Primer for Distinctive Debutantes." She has shared the secret for the perfect wedding gift.

**SHARDS OF GLASS IN YOUR EYE! #9 (MARCH 2013)**

Kari Tervo
P.O.B. 7831, Beverly Hills, CA 90212
shardsofglassinyoureye@gmail.com
www.etsy.com/shop/SweetMayhemZinery
Price: $3.00 / Trades: ask first
Size: 8.5" x 5.5" / Pages: 24 pages
Description: "nothing of consequence"

Another delightful issue featuring diary entries, notices of word discontinuations (what I like to call "vocabulary lessens," since Kari is recommending that we discontinue using some words—I agree with "hubby" and "preggers," but I the jury is out on "artisanal," which I haven't even gotten to try out yet).

In case anyone is deciding where to retire or vacation but has narrowed it down, there's a nice compare-and-contrast table of the Michigan Upper Peninsula and Los Angeles.

**SHARDS OF GLASS IN YOUR EYE! #15, MAY 2020**

Kari Tervo
P.O.B. 7831, Beverly Hills, CA 90212
shardsofglassinyoureye@gmail.com
www.etsy.com/shop/SweetMayhemZinery
Price: $3.00 / Trades: ask first
Size: 8.5" x 5.5" / Pages: 24 pages
Description: Run for the random, **SHARDS OF GLASS IN YOUR EYE! #15** is here! In **SHARDS #15**, have fun with essays about childhood malfeasance, quarantine fun, and festival life; hear me bitch about a common song misinterpretation, discover Paula Abdul's magical secret, and learn about a new psychological disorder. Among crookedly-placed pieces (I do try to make

them straight, I swear), solve some puzzles, ponder some hipster riddles, and enjoy juvenile vocabulary humor! Keep your pants off whether we're still in quarantine or not and settle in with **SHARDS #15**!

"A zine is making you laugh! I'm jealous. That's my job."

That was my husband's reaction as I was reading **SHARDS OF GLASS IN YOUR EYE!** I did enjoy this issue very much. I shouldn't be surprised that Kari lives in Beverly Hills, since in one place she calls herself "a fat person," but her photograph shows someone who is definitely not a fat person! Well maybe she just said that for the humorous (and insightful) joke, of which there are many.

Kari's description above sums up pretty well. Note that I was fully clothed as I read it; perhaps Kari's advice to keep your pants off will make you enjoy it even more, but in either case I had at least 6 syllables of laughter and a lot of smiling.

A couple of the jokes were over (or under) my head, but the ones that were at my level were very good. The job listing for the graphic designer for the city of L.A. makes this worth every penny (and that's only on page 3). I love the stories, and next time someone asks me "what's a zine?" I'll say **SHARDS OF GLASS IN YOUR EYE!**

**WATCH THE CLOSING DOORS #92**
Fred Argoff
Penthouse L, 1170 Ocean Parkway
Brooklyn, NY 11230
Price: $10.00 cash or a Winnipeg transit token / Trades: Yes
Size: 5.5" x 8.5" / pages 26

This is a special theme issue about buses. (By the way, I vote for this optional spelling of "buses" because "busses" can mean something else entirely. So I appreciated this issue within the first sentence.)

There are compelling photographs in here that make the whole thing worthwhile. See unusual bus stops, unusual vehicles from around the world, and a story that will make you understand why Fred wants cash only.

**1812 G Avenue #107**
**La Grande, OR 97850**
**pokiespout@gmail.com**

**DEAD DADS CLUB VOL #1**
Katherine Leung
754 The Alameda Apt. 4302,
San Jose CA, 95126
deaddadsclubzine@gmail.com
http://deaddads.club
Price: $12 / Trades: yes
Size: 5.5" x 8.5" / Pages: 42

The title may seem a bit cheeky, but **DEAD DADS CLUB** is a collaborative zine by a dozen writers and artists who are using the space to process the loss of a father or father-figure. And for these dozen contributors, there are at least that many ways of coping with grief – and the other, less predictable, emotions that surround such a significant event.

Photographs, prose, collage, and painting are all on display here, and the visuals are cleanly reproduced in full color. For a reader experiencing a recent or imminent loss of a parent, **DEAD DADS CLUB** would be a valuable collection of different perspectives and reactions. Check the web site for information on their second call for submissions! If you are seeking a way to process your own loss, knowing that the **DEAD DADS CLUB** exists might be the inspiration you need.

### BREAD OF THE RESISTANCE: HOW TO MAKE SOURDOUGH WITHOUT MEASURING

Tessalyn Morrison
Microcosm Publishing
2752 N Williams Ave., Portland OR, 97227
MicrocosmPublishing.com
Price: $9.99 USD
Size: 5.5" x 4.25" / Pages: 92

This zine is difficult to review, because whenever I open it to cite examples, or find particularly representative passages, I get sucked into it and wind up reading a dozen pages. What an amazing resource!

The primary goal of **BREAD OF THE RESISTANCE** is to gently demystify the concept of sourdough, to assure the reader that you (yes you!) are capable of making sourdough, and even turning it into a regular part of your life. Much of this is down to the author's tone, which is knowledgeable but not alienating. Sourdough may be outside your area of experience, but it isn't beyond your abilities!

I'm a baker, but I have never made sourdough, and part of the reason is that it seemed really complex (and sort of wasteful, with all the feeding and discarding). Tessalyn's descriptions made the process seem much more relaxed and forgiving, and she includes lots of ways to utilize the daily discarded portions of your starter.

As an incredible bonus, there are a number of unmeasured recipes for lots of great things like aioli, jam, kombucha, yogurt... luxuries and staples that you can make yourself and come to understand something about the essential nature of the foods we eat.

### BERLINER MAUERN #03

2018 or 2019?
neolivet@pm.me
https://berlinermauern.blog
Price: ? / Size: 5.5" x 8.5" / Pages: 44

The title translates to Berlin Wall, and the zine consists of crisply-reproduced black and white photographs of graffiti and street art in Germany. Little context is provided in the zine (perhaps more is available on the blog) but the photos themselves capture a variety of pictorial ventures. Traditional spraypainted tags, wheatpasted posters, sticker art and more adorn the pages of **BERLINER MAUERN**, and if you're the target market for this sort of thing, you probably already know that you want it!

### BERLINER MAUERN #04

summer 2019
bmzine@pm.me
https://berlinermauern.blog
Price: ? / Size: 4.25" x 5.5" / Pages: 28

I'm giving this issue of **BERLINER MAUERN** its own space, simply because it's so distinct from the previous issue. It is quite a lot smaller, but produced in full color on high-quality photo paper. This fourth issue focuses specifically on graffiti writing, as opposed to general street art: it's filled with examples of elaborately designed tags and phrases, some of which are in German. They're actually pretty amazing to look at, with tiny little glimpses of foreign cities peeking in around the edges. There is no indication of pricing for these issues, but they're both terrific (if you're into this sort of thing) and they came with posters and stickers and random photos included. It's really just what you want from a zine, and the fact that I don't speak German makes it all the more mysterious.

**RAZORCAKE #116 JUNE/JULY 2020**

PO Box 42129, Los Angeles CA, 90042
razorcake.org
Price: $3 / Size: 8.5" x 11" / Pages: 114

This long-running DIY punk magazine is probably familiar to many of you, and doesn't need a lot of help from me. As always, **RAZORCAKE** is packed with band interviews that go deeper than the music, which is why I usually enjoy them even though I'm not exactly the poster boy for punk fandom. What I love is punk people, and punk ethos, and the sort of raw energy and authenticity that permeates the best parts of punk culture, which is why I'm always drawn to that scene. This issue is, of course, published in the middle of a pandemic that has hit marginalized groups harder than anyone, so expect some heartfelt and appropriately political reaction to that (I'm writing this review on November 5th, after the US Presidential election took place but before the results have been tallied, and looking back over this issue makes me yearn for a simpler time when the Covid death toll was merely in the tens of thousands, and we could imagine that Americans might overwhelmingly vote against a burgeoning fascist regime).

Anyway, punks rule and their world is better than the one you live in, so you might as well read **RAZORCAKE** while Rome burns, right?

**THE KEN CHRONICLES #56**

Ken Bausert
2140 Erma Drive, East Meadow NY, 11554
Passscribe@aol.com
thekenchronicleszinesite.blogspot.com
Price: $3 US/ $3.50 Can/Mex/ $4 world /
Trades: yes / Size: 5.5" x 8.5" / Pages: 28

Classic perzine stylings from Ken Bausert, who spends much of this issue discussing his activities during the great Covid quarantine. **THE KEN CHRONICLES** (like, I suspect, many zines from this year) will someday make a fascinating historical database of how we all responded to the increasingly bizarre circumstances of 2020. This issue also pays tribute to people who have passed, things that have changed, and the importance of taking some time to finally read those comic books.

**NXOEED #1**

James B. Hunt
PO Box 1547, Phoenix AZ, 85001
csotys@gmail.com
jamesbhunt.com
Price: $6 US/ $7 Can/Mex/ $8 world /
Trades: maybe
Size: 8.5" x 7" / Pages: 32

The unpronounceable title of this zine is also the professional name/alter ego of James Hunt, a graphic artist from Arizona who I wish was my friend. His work is gorgeous, and the personality revealed in the zine is everything I love about the DIY world. He draws album covers and art show posters and comics, he photocopies them himself and distributes them by bicycle. He creates original artworks and hides them all around Phoenix and Tempe, for people to find and keep. He has art shows where people just pay what they can and take what they want. This is an artist who seems to create for the pure love of creating, and then moves on to create some more.

Even this zine, which gathers together tons of artwork that **NXOEED** created over the previous year, includes a whole section of "free art" for readers to utilize as they see fit. Want to have **NXOEED** create your next band poster, but don't want to bother with the trouble and expense of hiring him? Now you can cobble together your very own **NXOEED** poster, with his blessing!

You can't go wrong with this art zine, in glorious black and white, packed with gorgeous creatures and typefaces and even a Ham Thief. He is your new favorite artist and possibly your new best friend.

**FLUKE #17**

Matthew Thompson
PO Box 1547, Phoenix AZ, 85001
matthew@flukefanzine.com
flukefanzine.com
Price: $4 US, $5 Can/Mex/ $6 world /
Trades: maybe
Size: 8.5" x 5.5" / Pages: 52

Another great punk art zine, **FLUKE** is a collection of interviews, memoir, and enthusiastic celebration of culture and community. The second zine in my batch to include an interview with artist/musician Nate Powell, it covered completely different ground and I loved it. Many of the voices involved in this zine are people who are old enough to look back at their wild youth with such wonder, and appreciation, that it's hard not to get caught up in the nostalgia. You know how sometimes you remember something that you did as a kid, and you shake your head and think about how you could never do that now? Well, imagine if you had actually been cool and done awesome stuff when you were a kid! It's like that. They are people who have continued to live by the codes that defined them as adolescents, but evolved as artists and as human beings. Which is a great thing to see.

The interview with artist Danny Martin was a highlight for me. The way he talks about Tucson and its vibrant art scene, and the space he's made for himself within it, sounded pretty damn blissful. I wouldn't half mind finding something like that around here.

# index

# About us

If this is your first issue, **XEROGRAPHY DEBT** is a review zine for zine readers by zine writers. It is a hybrid zine review zine and personal zine. **XEROGRAPHY DEBT** is intentionally organized by reviewer and not by zine, because the reviews are coming from individuals.

Also, each reviewer "owns" the zine in a communal sense. We are individual artists and writers coming together to collaborate and help keep small press flourishing. Do your part by ordering a few zines from the many reviewed here and, if you self-publish, please consider including some reviews in your zine.

**XEROGRAPHY DEBT**'S reviews are selective. To explain the "system": Some reviewers choose to review zines they have bought or traded with, some review zines that are sent to **XEROGRAPHY DEBT** for review, and some do both.

Generally speaking, the only reviews you will read in here are "good reviews." Constructive criticism is given, but we don't have the time or money to print bad reviews. If you sent your zine in for review and don't see it listed, wait and see if it appears in the following issue (there are lags in our schedule and some reviewers don't get to everything right away). Occasionally mistakes happen, postal or otherwise, so if you have a question about a zine you sent in for review, please contact Davida at PO Box 347, Glen Arm, MD 21057 or davida@leekinginc.com.

You are also encouraged to join our Facebook group: https://www.facebook.com/groups/133821320262